RECLAIM YOUR POWER

Heal Trauma by Telling Your Story

JESSICA AIKEN-HALL

MOONLIT MADNESS
PRESS

Copyright © 2021 by Jessica Aiken-Hall

First Edition.

All rights reserved. No part of this publication may be reproduced, stored in any retrieval system, or transmitted, in any form or by any means, electronic, mechanical, photocopying, recording or otherwise, without the prior written permission of the author. If you would like permission to use material from the book (other than for review purposes), please contact http://jessicaaikenhall.com/contact

ISBN-13: 978-1-955071-02-4 (paper)

Library of Congress Control Number: 2021917889

Moonlit Madness Press

Cover Design © Shower of Schmidt Designs

https://showerofschmidtdesigns.com/

Editor: Proofreading By The Page

jessicaaikenhall.com

JESSICA AIKEN-HALL

HEAL TRAUMA BY TELLING YOUR STORY

Reclaim YOUR POWER

To everyone who has a story to tell. Now is the time to Reclaim Your Power.

Also by Jessica Aiken-Hall

The Monster That Ate My Mommy: A Memoir

Rebecca Remains: Shadow of a Doubt Book 1

Murder at Honeybee Lake: Shadow of a Doubt Book 2

Boundaries: Scope of Practice Book 1

Confidentiality: Scope of Practice Book 2

Accountability: Scope of Practice Book 3

House in the Woods

Contents

Introduction	xi
1. So, How Do You Reclaim Your Power?	1
2. Prepare Your Foundation	8
3. Open the Door to Self-Love	28
4. Work on Answering Some Important Questions Before You Begin	53
5. Explore Memories from Your Past	64
6. Release Your Secrets and Turn Your Memories into Stories	80
7. How to Write Through the Pain	94
8. Turn Your Memories into A Book	111
9. When You're Ready to Publish Your Story	137
10. Helping others	161
Acknowledgments	173
About the Author	175
Don't forget to grab your copy of the Companion Workbook!!	176

Introduction

"There is no greater agony than bearing an untold story inside you." **Maya Angelou**

Are you familiar with the agony Maya Angelou is speaking about? I was. It haunted me. I knew I had a story to tell, I just didn't know how to start. The more I wanted it, the more elusive it became. The words twisted around in my mind, but I couldn't figure out how.

Writing my memoir was something I knew I had to do. I knew I needed to get the past out of my head and onto paper. I didn't know where to start or how to begin. I spent years thinking about it, salivating at the idea of holding my very own book in my hands. But something kept stopping me. There was something in my way that wouldn't let me even begin.

I had a ton of excuses why I couldn't write it yet. My computer wasn't fast enough. I didn't have a laptop. I didn't have time. I had three kids. I worked a full-time

Introduction

job. I was my grandmother's caregiver. I was a full-time college student. You get the idea. I made a list of reasons at every turn that gave me permission to talk myself out of my dream.

When I bought a new computer, even a laptop, I still didn't write. When my kids started getting older and needed less of my attention, I still didn't write. When my gram passed away, I still didn't write. When I graduated from college, I still didn't write.

I grew tired with my excuses, but always had another one handy. It was how I could live with myself. I tried to talk myself into believing I didn't have a story to tell. That was the easiest one of all to believe. When I let my negative self-talk take over, there was no chance I'd ever be able to tell my story. The whispers of *"you don't even know how to write"* was what I heard the most followed for a close second of *"you don't even have a story to tell."* Truth is, writing has always been the one thing I've ever felt good at and turns out I had one hell of a story after all.

Have you ever thought about writing your story? The pieces of yourself you hide from the world. The parts of your past that visit you when you can't fall asleep. The story you have been gripping onto so tight, there are fingernail marks left behind.

I know the pain all too well of having a story to tell and not being able to get the words out. Maybe it's the lack of time, or faith, or ability that is keeping you from reaching your dream of telling your story. I'll tell you right now that's a load of crap. You have the time, and you have the ability. Fear is keeping your fingers off the keyboard and pen out of your hand.

Introduction

What would you say if I told you I know how to tell fear to STFU (shut the f*ck up)? What if I told you I can help you find the time to write? How about if I let you in on a little secret? You don't even have to know how to write to share your story. Say what?!?

That's right! Give me an excuse and I can help you slay it. I can help you reclaim your power by telling your story. Are you ready? Do you want to know what it takes to snatch your life back from the past that has been holding you hostage? Hang on, this could get bumpy!

In order for me to help you share your story, I have to tell you mine (at least the part that got me here in the first place).

I grew up in a home where I learned at a very young age I needed to keep secrets. Before I went to kindergarten, they made it clear that I could not share with anyone what went on at home. "What happens at home, stays at home." I took those words to the most literal extreme and soon became labeled as *painfully shy*. I didn't know what was okay to be shared and what wasn't, so I just said nothing.

The only bright spot in my life was my maternal grandmother. My earliest memories are of her reading to me, and later us reading together. She was my one source of unconditional love and gave me the strength to get through even the toughest days. Through my love of reading, I soon decided that I wanted to become an author. As a three-year-old, I can still remember gathering up paper and asking my gram to staple it together for me so I could make my book. Before I knew how to write, I filled the pages with pictures (mostly scribbles to start). When my book was complete, I would crawl into my gram's lap and tell her the story.

This desire to tell my story never dimmed. It became the light that kept me on my path on my darkest days. But the threat to not tell my secrets lingered with every breath I took. It became another one of my excuses.

As I got older, I had more stories to share. The abuse I endured as a child continued, although the perpetrators changed. The more years I lived; the more chapters I had to write. And yet they wouldn't come.

I focused my attention on my career and started working with the aging population as a case manager and later a social worker. After fifteen years working with death and dying, one thing remained steadfast; I wasn't the only one not sharing my story. I've sat at countless deathbeds and heard confessions that were too heavy to hold as they crossed over. Decades of trauma finally released, with minutes to spare.

As I sat and listened to these stories, my yearning to share my story intensified. The more I saw the weight lift from them when they released their secrets, the more I knew I needed to share my story. I didn't want to live my entire life still clinging to the trauma that had already stolen so much from me. I couldn't. There was something pushing me, not allowing me to give up.

I began writing my story in the fall of 2014. I had started a few times before this, but this was the first time I kept going. When I was about a quarter of the way into my story, I stopped. My fingers hovered over the keyboard and nothing more would come. After twenty-five thousand excruciating words, I couldn't go any further. Reliving the memories and trauma was too much. Way more than I imagined it would be. I hadn't even considered how much pain it would be to have to write about some of the most painful events in my life.

This setback was just one more push in believing I would never finish my story or hold a book I wrote in my hands. It fed the evil beast of negative thinking and stole my strength. Depression took a stronger hold as I watched the one thing I wanted wither away in front of me.

The stories from the clients I was working with continued. I watched the freedom of the release transform into them, and I knew I couldn't give up. Before I started writing my story, I had never sought help from the trauma I had experienced. I went to graduate school to heal myself. There had been one too many unpleasant experiences behind a counselor's door, and I didn't trust the profession.

A friend pushed me to work with a healer and I found myself with an intuitive Reiki Master, who was also the psychic medium I had visited over the previous decade. My time with her over the past ten years had replaced a therapist, so she knew much of my story. When things in my life didn't add up or became too heavy to hold, I went looking for answers from her, and later my gram after she passed away.

After a few weeks of sessions, she suggested I find a counselor. It was not what I wanted to hear, but I knew I was ready to uncover the pain. After months of working on my healing and uncovering my pain, I was ready to write my story again. The words fell out of me on to the screen, turning my first attempt into the first draft of my manuscript.

Fast forward to September 2017 when my memoir, *The Monster That Ate My Mommy* was published, and things got interesting. People from all over the country (and others, too!) were reading my story. I received feedback, reviews, emails and messages from readers. People who had their own story to tell were reaching out to me to tell me they knew what I had gone through and benefitted by learning they were not alone.

At book signings people came up to me and told me about their desire to write their story. They asked me how I did it and some even asked me to show them how. With help from a local photographer, we organized an event for domestic violence awareness month and helped thirty women share their stories. With their photo and a piece of their story out in the world, they found their voice and a sense of comradery; they were no longer victims of abuse, but now survivors.

I offered to teach a memoir writing course for a nonprofit organization for senior citizens when the demand became too much. When the class was over, it turned into a writer's support group as the members continued to work on their stories.

One seventy-five-year-old woman finished her memoir. It was a story that had haunted her all of her life, and when I watched her reclaim her power as she released her secrets, I knew I had to help as many people as I could share their stories.

Through the process of writing my story and helping many others share theirs, I have learned the steps needed

Introduction

in order to free yourself from the hold of your secrets. You don't even have to share your story with anyone to reclaim your power, all you need to do is get the words out of your head and onto the paper (or computer screen).

Are you ready to stop the excuses? I'm excited to share the steps that have helped me and countless others share our stories. If you're ready, the following pages will guide you to reclaiming your power and finding your voice.

You'll learn:

- How to get your foundation in place before you begin.
- The importance of self-care.
- Answer the questions why? How? And what?
- How to get the words out.
- How to shape your memories into stories.
- What do you do when it becomes too painful?
- What to do when you are ready to turn your stories into a book.
- What are your next steps (self-publish, find an agent, help other people share their stories)?

If you follow the steps outlined in this book, I know you will reclaim your power. You'll finally be able to trade in the shackles of your past for a superhero cape and crown! Are you ready to reclaim your power? I can't wait to see what is in store for you.

Introduction

But wait, are you in the right place?

Before we begin, let's talk a little about trauma. Maybe you're wondering if you've picked up the right book. I know you have, but in case you need to be convinced, let's talk about trauma. It seems to be on everyone's mind these days, whether we're talking about childhood trauma, or the trauma veterans experience. Believe me when I tell you there were many years I didn't think I had experienced trauma. I thought my experiences didn't qualify to be labeled with the T word. When I looked at what I had faced, I was quick to say it wasn't that bad. I knew others had faced much worse. There was no way I had a space with other trauma survivors on my own healing journey. There was no way my pain could measure up to theirs. I was wrong, and once I could understand that, I gave myself permission to heal the past hurts that had haunted me for so many years.

So, what is trauma anyway?

According to the American Psychological Association, **trauma** is an emotional response to a terrible event like an accident, rape, or natural disaster. This is a definition that had me believing the incidents I had experienced weren't *that bad*. I wasn't convinced they were *terrible* enough.

What I learned when I joined other trauma survivors at a week-long healing retreat was that the word terrible is what you make it. It doesn't have to be terrible to anyone else, only you. If what you experienced or

Introduction

witnessed altered your life in any negative way, you experienced trauma. There is no scale to measure one trauma against another.

I know I'm not the only one who has pushed away trauma and tried to shake it off as "not that bad," but in order to let go of it, we must acknowledge it. Was there a time in your life that something happened to you or someone you love and now things seem different? Did an event or action alter your life? Are you haunted by the past? Then, you have trauma. The event can be big or little. It can seem insignificant or monumental, but if it changed you or life as you knew it; it was trauma.

The time someone called you ugly in second grade and now you never feel pretty; that was trauma. The time when you were nine and your older brother called you fat, and now you have an eating disorder; that was trauma. The time you held the pillow over your head, so you didn't hear your parents fighting; that was trauma. The time when your boyfriend didn't listen to you when you said no; that was trauma (and rape). The time when you saw a horrific car accident; that was trauma. The time you lost someone you loved and life as you knew it changed; that was trauma. You get the idea. Trauma can be anything. It can happen to anyone, and it can happen any time.

What is traumatic for one person may not be traumatic for the next. We are all made differently, and the events that happen to us and around us shape us all differently. Own it. That's all you need to do. If it hurt, let it hurt and then release it.

Introduction

What happens when we don't own our trauma?

The answer to this question is different for everyone. For me, when I didn't own my trauma, I could not use my voice. I was timid and afraid. I was constantly waiting for the next incident to happen, the next person to hurt me. I wasn't living; I was barely surviving.

Unaddressed trauma can manifest into eating disorders, addictions, self-sabotaging behaviors, domestic violence, and much more. When trauma has a hold of you, your ability to live your life how you want to is next to impossible. We might mask our pain with pills or alcohol, or sex, or shopping, or food, but we will not be in control of our life; trauma will.

Are you ready to own your trauma? Learn what it is and where it came from? Are you ready to stop hiding from the past and face it head on? Then you are going to want to stick around because you found the right book (or it found you). Now that you're ready to embrace the pain and the memories, you are ready to get a solid foundation under you to begin the work ahead. I know you can do this, and I am incredibly proud of you for taking this first brave step.

1
So, How Do You Reclaim Your Power?

"The most common way people give up their power is by thinking they don't have any."
~Alice Walker

In order to reclaim your power, you will need to find your voice. Maybe it's been hidden for years, but if you're ready and follow the steps outlined in this book, you will uncover it. My hope for you is that once you locate your voice, you'll embrace it.

The first step in taking your power back is letting go of the secrets and shame that have been preventing you from telling your story. It's time to let go of the fear and take control of your story. When you decide you're ready to share your story, you're the one in control. Not the words or the people you've been protecting—just you. You have the ability to share or just release the words.

When you take your power back by sharing your

secrets, you gain the control of your story, and ultimately your life. You're the one who can rewrite your future, taking back the hold the past has over you. The trauma that once kept you hostage, will now bring you freedom.

When I released parts of my story, I felt a shift within myself. It reintroduced me to the parts of me I had forgotten about. I could peel layers away and really see who I was. It was a messy process in the beginning, but that was before I learned the needed steps that are in this book. When I began to write my story, I was exhausted and angry. The hurt I had buried for so many years bubbled up to the surface, and I had a hard time pushing it all back in.

Let me introduce you to the P.O.W.E.R. method.

- **P**repare your foundation.
- **O**pen the door to self-love.
- **W**ork on answering some important questions before you begin.
- **E**xplore memories from your past.
- **R**elease your secrets and turn your memories into stories.

I used the P.O.W.E.R. method and released the hold my past had over me. I took the time to get my support system in place and worked on my safety plan. Then I looked at what I needed to do to take care of myself. I spent some time getting to know who I was and what I needed to succeed.

I went over some questions that needed to be answered to help me understand why I wanted to tell my story, and why I hadn't told it yet. I went over my memories and decided what I wanted to include and what I wanted to let go of. Then, with all the strength I gathered from the earlier steps, I could write and release my secrets and turned them into my memoir.

It sounds simple, I know, but trust me when I tell you there is much more to it than that. In order to let go of the secrets, some we don't even know we have, it takes a lot of work; physically and emotionally. You must be ready to let go of the safety net of not owning your own power. You must become vulnerable. You must relearn who you are and be ready to embrace who you will become.

The thing is, I didn't know what to do. I didn't know how to take my power back from the words that were haunting me. I was allowing the old hurt and trauma to hold the power. I could not overcome the demons of the past. It was as if the past was holding me hostage. It was not allowing me nutrition, water, or light. It sat upon me, making it next to impossible to climb out from under. But I did. I found a way, and in 2017 my memoir was published, and I released my secrets.

How did I crawl out from under the layers of doubt and self-sabotage? I created the process discussed on the following pages to tell my story. Since sharing my story, I have had the honor of helping many others share their stories, as well. Not only have I experienced the freedom of releasing my past, but I have seen others reclaim their power as they turned their secrets into stories.

The process is as simple or as complex as you would like to make it. You can go as deep as you are willing, or you can scratch the surface. How much you want to release is up to you. Who you share your story with is up to you. The beauty of this is you are in control of your story now. Once you reclaim your power, you can do what you wish with it.

The first step involves getting your foundation in place before you delve into the past you need to be released from. This is the most important step, because without it, you set yourself up for failure. If you do not have a solid foundation underneath you, when you move forward, you might fall like a stack of cards. It may seem silly at first to do this work, but it is necessary before you get in too deep.

The past, and the stories we have kept hidden, pack a punch. You might think you are okay, or even healed from your past trauma, but chances are there is some unfinished business lingering in the background. It might be the slightest memory that can knock you off your feet. You must do the work to be prepared for whatever comes your way.

The next step involves taking care of you. How long has it been since you were kind to yourself? In chapter three, you will learn ways to take care of your mind, body, and soul. Without this step, it is easy to forget why you are doing this in the first place. You deserve to be kind to yourself. It's time you become a priority in your own life.

Once you have taken the time to build your foundation and care for yourself, it is time to answer some questions. Before you go too deep into your story, it is important to understand your 'why' for sharing. Do you want to let go of your story strictly to heal yourself? Will your story be for your eyes only? Or will you share it with friends and family or is the plan to publish your book and help others? The answer to these questions can change over time. Maybe you want to write to heal and then get to a place where you are strong enough to share your story with family and then others. It can also go the other way, where your intentions were to write your memoir, but you decided you are not ready for that. As I said before, and I will say again, ***you are in control of your story now.***

We will move on to answering the questions of how and what. How will you share your story? We will go over the various ways to get the words from inside your head and onto the paper (or video or voice recording). We will discover the different ways your project can take shape and what it may look like. You have so much freedom in this section everyone can walk away with a different version. This is where your voice and your vision come alive.

After you have answered these questions, it is time to turn your memories into stories. As with the previous step, this can be achieved in many ways. You can pick what you share and what you leave out. You will learn different ways to accomplish the task at hand.

As with everything that is worth doing in life, it is now when we might find it too difficult to continue. Giving up is your option, but you will be given tools to keep going even when it feels like you cannot. This is the time where you will harness your power you have been working so hard for. The tools from the previous steps will come in handy as you learn how to push through the painful process. You will walk away straightening your cape and adjusting your crown.

The last few chapters leave you with more questions and opportunity. If after sharing your story you want to turn it into a book, and even publish it, you will learn how to take these steps. You may even want to use what you have learned and help others reclaim their power. You will learn what is needed to turn your knowledge into power. You'll be kicking ass and taking names (of the people who need what you know).

Each chapter will include exercises to help get you on your way and introduce new (or refresher) concepts. You will also find **power hints** to give you some helpful pointers and **power prompts** to help get your creativity flowing. Everything included is optional. If something is too far out of your comfort zone, or you don't feel it will be helpful, skip it. Get used to being in control. This is your story!

If this sounds like something you are ready for, all you need is an open mind and willing heart. This won't be easy, but it will be worth it. You have so much to give. Why not start by giving yourself the freedom to reclaim your power? You've got a story to tell!

Power Hint: Pick out a journal you love, one that you'll be excited to write in. While you're at it, find some special pens! Nothing helps get your creativity flowing like using new writing tools!

Power Prompt: What is your hope for telling your story?

2

Prepare Your Foundation

"You have the power to heal your life, and you need to know that. We think so often that we are helpless, but we're not. We always have the power of our minds... Claim and consciously use your power." ~Louise Hay

It's amazing to think about the power we all harness inside ourselves; without even trying. It just exists, filling our crevasses until we are ready to unleash it. Some of us figure this out sooner than others, but if you look close enough, you'll see it. Every one of us has what we need to survive. Think back to a time in your life, to a time where you were at your lowest. Now think about what led you out of that space. **You**. Even if you had help to guide you, you were still the one responsible for the liberation. When you feel like giving up, stop and remember how far you have come. That alone should be enough to push you along the expedition of life.

Writing your story can often lead you down some dangerous, lonely roads. These are destinations that we have spent our life hiding from, maybe even pretending they don't exist. When we dig up the past, we are at risk of awakening the trauma. It may have been years since we looked at the events in our lives and allowed them to touch us. When we are at the point of knowing we are ready to let go of the pain, it is time we get some very important things in place.

When I began writing my story, I was ill-equipped. I knew I wanted to write my story, but that was all I knew. I didn't know where to begin or what to expect. I experimented with a few ideas and then tucked it away. The pain from the past would not let me continue. At this time in my life, I had not begun my healing journey. I didn't know I needed one. I figured that once I wrote my story it would be over and done with. My past would become something I no longer needed to worry about. I could wash my hands of it and walk away. I was wrong.

I had not stepped foot in a counselor's office in over twenty years, and I had not talked about my trauma or how to heal the pain from my past. I wanted to write my story, but I didn't fully understand what that would entail. In my mind I was *healed* from the incidents in my past; there was no way they could hurt me now. When memories came up, I quickly tucked them away, but not before patting myself on the back for being "over it." Over it? Reading it now, the absurdity of the claim heats my cheeks. I would never expect someone else to get over what had caused them pain, surely not before they had a chance to work through it. But that was what I expected from myself. I was under the notion that if I tucked it away and didn't let myself feel any of the pain, I was good to go.

When I began my healing work, I learned the reason I was so good at tucking things away was because of my Post Traumatic Stress Disorder (PTSD). The PTSD left me numb to the pain, but it also left me numb to the joy. When I didn't take the time to feel the pain, I wasn't prepared to experience other emotions. I was a slave to the act of running from my past. I wasn't facing it, but I wasn't living, either. I had set myself up for failure.

The trauma that I was running from was not allowing me to heal. How can you heal when you haven't even faced it? It made perfect sense in the moment; no attention makes things wither away. Without air or attentiveness, it could not grow. Wrong (again). See, trauma is a funny beast. Unlike most things, the more we neglect our trauma, the stronger and more powerful it becomes. Soon that little rock I had buried my past hurt under could no longer hide it. I traded the rock in for a boulder, and then a mountain. The pebble I could once kick out of the way became a mountain I was not equipped to climb. My shoes didn't have any traction, I ran out of trail mix, and my canteen was bone dry.

It took me twenty-five thousand words into my first attempt at my memoir before I understood just how much it could hurt. The pain was paralyzing. I could not continue writing my story, and reliving my past took my breath away. I was at a standstill and the trauma I thought I had healed from was slapping me across the face, telling me it wasn't finished with me. All those years of hiding it caught up with me. Ready or not.

I didn't have a lot of people I could share this experience with. The person who had caused most of my trauma was my mother, and she wasn't the ideal person to go have a conversation with about how the pain was swallowing me whole. I was used to internalizing stuff and letting it pile up inside me. The further down memory lane I went, the deeper I fell into depression.

I didn't understand at the time how important it was to get things into place before diving into the past. Words are not just words when they carry so much pain. The following year I started taking small steps, getting my foundation in place. I worked with a Reiki Master and a counselor. I also started sharing with my friends all the secrets I had been holding for so long. For the first time in my life, I was in a healthy, safe relationship and I could share with my partner, as well.

As I started getting all the secrets from the past uncovered and out into the open, I could start working on the healing process. A large part of this process was learning how to love myself. As someone who grew up being torn apart at the seams, this was a lot harder than just saying the latest catch phrase from a self-help book. I had to go deep. So deep that I had to awaken my inner child and learn what *she* needed. What did that four-year-old little girl who had her life threatened by her father need? What did the five-year-old little girl need when her mom was neglecting her?

In order to get the strength needed to continue my story, I had to do the work. I learned this the hard way, and I am hopeful you will take what I learned and have a smoother journey into the past. Take the time to go through the exercises in this book (even if they seem silly!) and get everything in order so you'll be able to take the control back from your past and your trauma.

Who is your support system?

Before you even begin putting your fingers to the keyboard to start your story, take a moment and think about this question. *Who is your support system?* Who can you go to if you are struggling as you awaken your past?

Think about the people you can trust. Who are the people you can go to when you are sad, lonely, or depressed? Are you currently working with a therapist? If not, is it something you would consider? Do you know of the number or website for the crisis hotlines for suicide, domestic violence, mental health or any other area you might struggle with? Do you have a family member you trust who you would be able and willing to talk with? Is this someone who might have also experienced the issues you will write about? Would this be helpful, or would it be triggering if your memories do not match up?

Do you have friends, either in your life or online, that are available if you need them? Would you be comfortable sharing with these friends if something comes up and you need help? Do you have a good relationship with your doctor? Would you be able to reach out to him or her if you need help? Would you call if things started feeling overwhelming?

The size of your list doesn't matter. For this exercise,

it is quality and not quantity that counts. Trust issues go hand in hand with past trauma, so it's even more important to make sure you have someone you can lean on and ask for help if you need to. Writing can be very lonely. Now is not the time to isolate. Reach out and ask for help when you need it.

Take a few minutes and copy the list below on paper, or some place you will have access to later. Now fill out as much of the list as you can.

Exercise:
My Support Team

My best friend:
My partner or spouse:
My therapist:
My doctor:
A family member I trust:
The crisis hotline:
The hospital:
My neighbor:

Keep this list in a place you can access when you need it and come back to it if you begin to feel overwhelmed by the process. Reliving past trauma can get messy, but you do not have to do it alone. Say it with me: "I am not alone. I am not alone. I am not alone."

Safety

As a survivor of domestic violence, sexual abuse,

child abuse (the list goes on and on), I know all too well what it feels like to worry about my safety. Living with PTSD safety is always on my mind. Before you begin writing, it should be on yours, too.

When I talk about safety, I am talking about your physical and emotional safety. Each is important to consider before you dive into your past traumas. As you let down the walls to your past, you must be prepared for what might come. The best-case scenario you won't need to use any of the strategies listed, but it is always wise to be over-prepared when it comes to safety. Like they say, it's better to be safe than sorry.

Physical Safety

If you still live or are in contact with a person (or people) from your past that have caused you harm, your number one priority is to make sure you are safe. If you have not developed a safety plan now might be a good time to think of one. If you do not have anyone who can help you with this, there are domestic violence advocacy groups online, and maybe even in your community that can help you. The number one rule is to trust your instincts. You know your situation better than anyone else, so if something they suggest doesn't sound doable, don't risk your safety.

If you feel that writing about situations involving your abuser won't be helpful in your healing process, save that piece to write about when you are able or leave it out completely. Make sure they do not have access to your writing; this includes your journal, your notes, your story, or the research you have done online. If you want to share your writing with them, this needs to be your choice, it should not be something that is out of your control. Chances are if an abusive person finds your writing (especially if you have written about them) it might ignite their anger, causing them to become dangerous.

Please be cognizant of your surroundings as you write. If you do not want people to read your work without your permission, consider getting a thumb drive and saving your work to that and make sure you take it with you at all times. If you use a journal or notebook to write in, please consider where you are leaving it and keep it in a safe location or bring it with you when you leave the house. There are also programs that allow you to have a digital journal that is password protected.

These suggestions are not to provoke paranoia, but to use as you plan for your safety. You are the one who knows your circumstances and you will know the precautions you should take. Take some time to consider your safety before you begin writing.

Physical safety is also important to consider if depression or suicidal thoughts creep in. The past can stir up a great deal of emotion for many of us. If you begin to feel unsafe, or like you may cause harm to yourself (or someone else), please use the list of your support team and reach out for help. Asking for help does not make you weak. It is quite the opposite. Reaching out for help when you need it is incredibly brave and takes a tremendous amount of courage. Please take the time you need to be in a safe place before you continue with your story.

It may take you longer to get the words out, but you will be taking the needed steps to heal the trauma from your past.

Your Safe Place

If you have ever been in counseling, chances are you have created your safe place. This is a place that you create in your mind that brings you peace and safety. It is a place where you can go when you are feeling overwhelmed by emotion. When you are in this place, you are safe.

This place can be made up, or it can be a place you have been to in the past. It can be at the ocean, the forest, or even your childhood bedroom. It can be anywhere you can escape the pain. The place you create should not cause you panic or harm. It should leave you with a sense of safety and calm.

To find your safe place, close your eyes and let your mind take you on a trip. What do you see? Let the visions come and don't force anything. Maybe what you see is not what you expect but go with it. Your unconscious mind will know where to take you.

When I created my safe place with my counselor, I was determined I was going to walk along the ocean. This is the place that brings me the most joy, and I felt it was where I should be going. I was wrong. When I would try to force myself into this space, I didn't feel the comfort and safety I was seeking. Instead, it brought me more stress and anxiety. When I let my mind lead me, I ended up in the forest. It was a place I used to go as a child, one that I had forgotten about. Now, when I close my eyes and call upon this place, it comes. I feel a blanket of calm come over me.

Exercise:
Create your safe place

Give it a try. Close your eyes and take a deep breath. As you exhale, notice where you are. What is around you? What do you hear? What do you smell? What do you feel? Are you alone or is someone with you?

Let the safety of your surroundings take away the fear or sadness the memories evoked for you. You are in control. You are safe. Let the sounds and smells from your safe place flow through you as you soak in the safety. Nothing can hurt you in your safe place. You are free from the memories. You are free from the people who caused you harm.

Close your eyes and let your mind take you to a place you feel safe. Once you find this place, reflect on how it makes you feel. Recognize the feeling of safety it brings you. Notice any smells or sounds that are in this safe place. *This is your safe place.*

You can go to this place any time that you need. When, after writing, talking, or even thinking about your past trauma, you can travel back to this safe place. Let the safety of your surroundings take away the fear or sadness the memories evoked for you. You are in control. You are safe. Let the smells and sounds from your safe place flow through you as you soak in the safety. You can go to this place any time you feel overwhelmed by the process.

Take a few moments to write or draw your safe place. Include the location, the sights, sounds, and smells that brought you comfort and safety. Come back to this when you need a reminder.

Is there a word or phrase you think of when you are in this safe place or will help you get to this safe feeling quickly?

My safe word or phrase is:

After you have spent some time in your safe place, notice how you feel. For me, I notice a warm sensation flow through my body. As you write, or even think about some events from your past, remember you can go to your safe place at any time. When you are in your safe place, you leave the troubling thoughts and memories behind. Nothing can hurt you there. You are the queen (or king) of your safe place. You call the shots. Call upon this place whenever you need.

Your Safe Space

When you are writing about past trauma, it is important to have a safe space within your home you can go to and work. For some of us, we need structure when we write, others can curl up on the couch with their laptop with their favorite TV show on in the background. The area needs to be a location where you feel safe and comfortable and needs to be a place you can access quickly. It can be inside your home or outside. Whatever you need, honor yourself with listening to what will work best for you.

You can clean this space before you begin writing to make it how you feel most comfortable. You can also cleanse the space with sage or incense. Once this space is how you want it, you can add things to help you feel grounded and comfortable. Scented candles, essential oil, photos of people, places, or items that bring you joy might help create the atmosphere you desire. Fill your space with any items that bring you happiness and comfort. You can also keep the space clear. Make it yours. Make sure there is nothing in this space that will take your focus away. Keep bills, paperwork, or unfinished projects out of this area. Having this safe space will help you as you relive the past trauma. As you look around, it will remind you that you are safe and in control. A space where you feel comfortable will also help with your creative flow. Even if you don't always work in this space, having it available will help you stay grounded when you are feeling overwhelmed.

Look around your home and see if there is a space you can dedicate to your writing. If you use an office space or desk, make sure there are no other stress provoking items in your workspace, such as bills or to-do lists. Turn your space, no matter how small, into your sanctuary.

Self-talk

Now that you have your safety taken care of, it is time to think about your mental health safety. What better place to start than with self-talk! This is one of the most powerful weapons or allies we have for ourselves. Self-talk is just as it sounds—it is what you say to yourself. It is the internal dialogue that plays in your head. Your words hold power; what you say and what you think.

When the same loop of words repeats in our heads it's hard not to believe them. Typically, we are our own worst critics so the words we say to ourselves are often unkind. Breaking the toxic self-talk train of thought can be hard and it can take a lot of practice. Without thinking too much about it, what are some things you say to yourself?

"You don't even know what you're talking about," is a big one for me. Hell, as I write this, I have to keep telling these thoughts to take a hike! There are plenty others that take up residency in my head. "You're so disgusting." "You're so lazy." "You can't do anything right." These thoughts are often words we have heard before from others and they are things we begin to believe about ourselves. I mean, how could we not? So, think about how easy it was for you to believe something unkind about yourself. The good news is if you can believe the unkind words, you can also believe the kind words.

These thoughts become how we see ourselves. They allow us to accept treatment from others we do not deserve. If we do not see ourselves as worthy, chances are no one else will, either. Our power will not truly shine when we are busy tearing ourselves down. We need to take the time to build ourselves up.

What does this have to do with telling your story? Everything. Think about the stories you tell yourself about the past. Now, think about how you paint yourself in those stories. If you want to reclaim your power, start with the power from within. When you take loving care of yourself, you will feel your inner self strengthen. You are no longer your own worst enemy.

Exercise:

Write a list of every negative thing you can think of that you tell yourself. Think of the messages that play on repeat in your head. Once your list is complete, go back and write a second list with a positive statement that is self-accepting and loving to counteract each negative message.

Example*:*
Negative: I am a failure.
Positive: I do the best that I can.

After you have each phrase changed, pick a couple to focus on. When you hear yourself say the negative words in your head, stop yourself and change the words to something positive. Continue to do this each time you are aware of the thoughts that enter your mind. It will take time and practice, but soon you will see your thought process change.

When working on your self-talk look at it this way, would you say the things you repeat in your head to a child or to your grandmother? If your answer is *no*, then don't say it to yourself. Let that be a guide for how you treat yourself from now on. If you cannot imagine saying those things to a child or someone you love, do not say them to yourself.

Journaling

Do you write in a journal? Some people are faithful journal writers. Everything that happens in their life ends up between the pages of their journal. There is a reason journaling has been gaining popularity. It's because it helps. Having a space to unload thoughts and record memories is a powerful tool in the healing process.

Even people who have trusted people they can talk to keep a journal. This is a place where secrets live. It's a safe place to process emotions. Things that wind up in a journal may never be spoken. A journal is the perfect place to keep your deepest, darkest secrets—the ones you never have to speak.

Writing in a journal can be a therapeutic release. When you feel overwhelmed with thoughts, try putting them onto paper. Get a journal or notebook specifically for this purpose. Notice how you feel after the words flow through your fingers and land on the page. When you free your mind of these thoughts you open yourself up to healing. Journaling can help you work through an issue that would otherwise ferment inside your head. When you rid yourself of the toxins, your body begins to heal.

Try to make writing in your journal part of your daily routine. And I know what you're thinking. I can hear you from here. "But I have to write my story, I don't have time to journal." I get it but trust me. Even if you begin to just write a sentence or two each day, make it a habit. You'll be surprised at what comes to the surface.

Tips for journaling:

- Just write, don't overthink it.
- Let your unconscious mind guide you.
- Keep everything you write. You never know when it might come in handy.
- Keep your journals in a safe place if you are concerned people will invade your privacy.

Support Groups

Support groups can be very helpful when you are looking to come together with others who share similar experiences. Depending on where you live, support groups may be available for a variety of topics. If you live in a more rural area (like I do), you may need to travel to find a support group you are looking for, or there might not be one offered. You have a couple of options in this situation. You can either start your own support group or you can go online. These days there is a support group for most everything online.

When I was writing my memoir, which covered topics of child abuse, sexual assault, grief and loss, domestic violence and mental illness, I started searching online for groups I could join. I am still a member of a few of these groups where there are like-minded people who have experienced some things I have. It was a great support as I relived some of my trauma. There were people I could talk to who understood where I was coming from and how I was feeling. These strangers became friends who offered support and a nonjudgmental space.

Not all groups are created equal so you will need to search around. You will want to make sure you feel safe in the group and you will want to find out what the rules of the group are. A safe group will at the very least ask that all members practice confidentiality; what is shared in the group stays in the group. If you find yourself feeling uncomfortable in the group listen to your instincts. If you do not feel you are able to share or that listening to other members is not helpful give yourself permission to move on.

If you cannot find a good fit in an existing support group and you want to start your own, reach out to a couple other people who are experiencing the same issues or trauma that you have. Together you can work on the details, find a space, and come up with a set of group rules and guidelines. If there is no one in the group who is trained, be sure to let other members know the group is a peer support group. A search online will give you some tips and pointers and depending on the topic of your group, there might be an organization that will offer you support along the way.

Writing Communities

Much like support groups, writing communities are full of support and friendship. Not all groups are created equal, but if you do a little research, you will find some very supportive people who love to write. When I began writing my memoir, I had no idea what I was doing. All I knew was that I needed to get my story out. I had no idea there was a glorious community of other writers who came together to share tips and offer support and advice. This was one of my greatest finds.

All of the groups that I joined I found on social media, and many of them I have been a part of for years. One perk of joining these communities is that once you are a member, you can search previous topics. There are endless amounts of information, and if you spend some time looking through posts, you will walk away with at least one new piece of information. The next time you're endlessly scrolling through social media, hop into a writing group of your choosing and let your brain absorb some new information.

I have seen some genuine, lasting friendships form in these groups. I've made friends that I cherish from the groups I am in. Writers are some of the kindest people I have met and the commitment they have to each other is unwavering. I have learned so much from people who have been where I am, and I know you will, too. Before long, these are some friends you can add to your support team list. A quick search for nonfiction or memoir writers will give you enough results to keep you busy for a while!

Triggers

Before you begin writing your story, it will be helpful if you consider your triggers. These triggers may be from an event or from a person. For some of us, we will know without a doubt what our triggers are. It is possible that we have a trigger (or more) that we are unaware of. For me I knew some of my triggers and prepared myself for them by holding off on writing about that topic, but there were others that snuck up on me. They took my breath away, and at the moment I wasn't even sure what had happened.

If you are aware of what your triggers are, there are some tools you can use to work through them before they take on a life of their own. We can also use these tools to work through the triggers that catch us off-guard.

As you write about and remember the traumatic events from your past, you may find certain events, people, or things are triggers. When you can take control of these triggers, the trauma loses some of its power and control over you.

Some ways to manage your triggers include:

- breathing exercises
- meditation
- avoiding extra stress
- talking with supportive friends, family, or professionals

The goal is to manage the trigger and take control of the situation. It is okay to still have the negative emotions related to the event.

Once you have your foundation in place, you are ready to move on to the next step. Make sure you take the time you need in each step. Don't rush the process. Your story has waited for you this long, it will wait a little while longer while you make sure you are safe in your body and your mind. For some of us making ourselves a priority is uncomfortable and uncharted territory. Think about how you would feel if someone you love was treated how you have been treating yourself. Make yourself matter as much as the people you love. You are training others how to treat *you*.

You are worth it. You matter. Your story matters.

Repeat after me: *"I am worth it. I am in control of my story. I reclaim my power."*

Power Hint: Pick your favorite quotes, self-affirmations, or sayings and write them on sticky notes or index cards and leave them around your house where you will see them.

Power Prompt: What would your perfect day entail?

> 3
>
> Open the Door to Self-Love

"Take a risk. You have the power within to move mountains." ~Cheryl Richardson

Before you get into the depths of your past, it is important to continue to take the steps to make sure you are ready to dredge up the past trauma. Trauma has a sneaky way of catching us off guard, but if you take the steps before you begin, you will be in a much better space to do the work that is coming.

When I started writing my memoir, before I used the P.O.W.E.R. method, I didn't do the needed work and I could not continue. The trauma ate me alive, and I didn't have any tools to fall back on. Without the tools in place, depression took a hold of me and I wanted to give up. It was easier. My story waited, but it didn't stop tapping me on my shoulder. The desire didn't go away, it just led me down the path I should have been on in the first place.

Some areas I needed to work on included self-care,

forgiveness, and setting boundaries. As someone who was used to being treated with disrespect and abuse, it was easy to add myself to the list of repeat offenders. My self-worth was close to nonexistent. This was further proof I needed to take the time for myself.

Louise Hay was one of the founders of the self-help movement. She spent much of her adult life helping other people learn how to heal their lives and learn to love themselves. The techniques she used in her teachings have helped millions of people. Louise's work inspired much of what is covered in this chapter. She was motivational and what she taught makes sense.

When I read her books, I notice myself nodding, agreeing with her. She, like us, lived a tormented childhood. I felt a tear roll down my cheek when I heard her tell her story. I was listening to an audiobook which was narrated by her. In her own words, I heard where she had been and could understand the magnitude of the transformation she had undergone to be where she was in that moment. Chills ran down my spine as I soaked in her words. She was not much different than I was. She knew the pain I had experienced, and she didn't give up. She kept on going and meeting her goals and turning her dreams into her reality.

When I knew Louise knew what she was talking about, because she'd been where I had been before, I knew I had found her work for a reason. I felt a deeper connection to Louise after I heard her story. I knew more than ever I needed to help others find the strength to share their story. By releasing her story, she could heal her life and, in turn, she helped so many others. Even though she passed away in 2017, her work is still helping those who find it. Her passion for her work and all she believed in makes me aspire to do this work. There are no coincidences and that's how I know you have the right book. Something inside you called you to pick it up. And now, we've got work to do.

Are you ready? If you try to address everything all at once, there is a good chance you will fail, so pick an area you need to work on and start there. If you want to succeed, you must do the work upfront. If taking care of your needs is new to you, start out small. Just do one thing at a time.

Self-love

What does that even mean? Obviously, it means you need to love yourself, but what does that mean? Self-love was something I was resistant to. I didn't understand why it was so hard for me to love myself. My counselor and Reiki healer gave me homework with specific instructions to learn what I needed to accept love from myself. I smiled when I received the assignment and then rolled my eyes so much on my drive home I got a migraine.

The thought of what they were asking me to do seemed so simple, yet impossible. One exercise they gave me was to look at myself in the mirror and just say, "I love you." Easy enough, right? Not for me. I stood in front of the mirror and I couldn't even make eye contact with myself, and there was no way I could say those words. Not to myself. I couldn't understand why it was so hard. Not until I worked through a lot of stuff.

Long story short is words matter to me, especially those words. I was married to my first husband for seven years and I never once told him I loved him, because I didn't. Love was such a scarcity in my life that it became almost sacred. I couldn't throw the words around without meaning. I'm true to my word, to a fault sometimes, and this wasn't an exception. I couldn't say the words, not even to myself, because I didn't believe them.

When the reality of that settled around me, I was finally able to look in my eyes and watched myself cry. My eyes turned red and my vision blurred with moisture. "You can't even love yourself? How pathetic."

I stopped myself and my negative self-talk in their tracks. It wasn't pathetic; it was sad. If I wasn't able to love myself, it was no wonder I was attracting people in my life who were hurting me. I wasn't valuing myself, and no one else was, either. I wiped the tears out of my eyes and closed them tight. When I opened them again I said, "I love you." I held my gaze long enough to watch the pain slip away. When I walked out of the bathroom, I felt things shift. It didn't seem so foolish to love myself. I needed it more than ever.

Self-love is a word that gets thrown around a lot. It seems to be part of every self-help practice out there, but for good reason. Self-love is the heart of self-care; without it you'll be building yourself up on a hollow base that has the potential to topple over at any second.

So, what is self-love? It looks different for everyone, but the premise is that you love and accept yourself unconditionally. The first step is to let go of the idea that you have to be perfect. Perfection is an illusion, and the cost of chasing it is never worth the reward. Trade perfection in for progress and honor the work you are doing.

Stop comparing yourself to others. You are unique. Learn to be grateful for your uniqueness. Spend less time on social media, which has become a breeding ground for self-doubt. What you see posted online is just the tip of the iceberg. You don't know the entire story, so it's not fair to compare yourself to other people's situations. You are worth more than that.

Live in the present moment. Try to let go of the regrets from your past. You cannot change anything that has already happened, all you can do is learn from it. On the flip side, don't spend time worrying about what is going to happen. Trust that you will have what you need when you need it.

Be grateful. When you show gratitude for the things you have, you will find more things to be grateful for. If you live in a state of negativity, you will find more of the same. The same holds true when you find the good in situations, more will follow. Maybe life isn't how you expected it to be, but find reasons to be grateful for what you have. This will change your life. The dark cloud that follows you will move out of the way for the sunshine.

Take small steps to honor yourself. Treat yourself how you would treat other people you care about. You deserve the same love and respect you give others. Loving yourself doesn't have to be difficult. Embrace yourself, everything about you. You are worthy of love, especially your own.

Mirror work

A great tool to help encourage self-love is mirror work. This is a concept Louise Hay taught and has been helpful for many people. The idea is to stand in front of your mirror and talk to and get to know yourself. It is uncomfortable and challenging at first as you look into your eyes. Let whatever comes come, even if it's positive. Keep note of what is said so you know where you need to focus your attention.

When I first did this, I was critical of almost every aspect of myself. If I could see it, I found a flaw. "Your nose is too big." "Your eyebrows are too bushy." "Where did that hair come from?" When I stopped long enough to look into my own eyes, I could see past all of that. I could see the hurt my criticism was causing.

The next day I didn't let the critical words come. Instead, I told myself, "I love your eyes." "You have a welcoming smile." I fought through the desire to be cruel to myself and found something kind to say. Each day I did this, it became easier. And the person in the mirror was no longer a stranger. She became my friend.

This is a powerful exercise that can help you get to know yourself. It might be uncomfortable in the beginning, but the reward at the end is worth it. If you would like to learn more about this Louise Hay wrote a book *Mirror Work: 21 Days to Heal Your Life* that will teach you all you need to know about the process.

Self-care

Talk of self-care is everywhere, but how many people actually take care of themselves? Most people spend their days too busy to do anything extra. They work and have a family and home to take care of. And now add writing your story to the mix. I can already hear it... (insert whiny voice here) "There's no way I have any extra time."

I get it, I really do. It took me a long time to put myself first. It came down to not having a choice. Either I continued on with the insane schedule of taking care of everyone else and watch myself fall apart or find a way to stop. The thing is, if you really want something, you'll find a way. Think about all the things you do for other people and what you go through to make sure they're taken care of. Now I want you to apply that effort to your own needs, and not even all that much. Just enough to make sure your needs are met.

We live in a society that sends us mixed messages; we have to do it all for everyone and we have to stop at nothing to make sure it happens all while we're told we need to practice self-care. But how do you do that? How do you find even five minutes for yourself? That was my excuse. I didn't have the time, and I'd tell you that as I mindlessly scrolled through social media or zoned out on TV. Now, if those were activities that were bringing me joy and not causing me to avoid what I really should have been doing, I could have been practicing self-care. But it was neither. It was an escape from my life, from my exhaustion, and from the shame of not taking care of me.

I figured if I didn't have enough time or enough money, there was no point in doing anything for myself. The money could be better spent on the kids or I could use the time to take the kids to the movies. There was always an excuse, always a reason why I didn't deserve to indulge in self-care. This all changed for me when I understood self-care wasn't selfish. If I was taking care of myself, I was in a better space to take care of the people I love. By taking care of me, I could take better care of the people around me. I was saving time and energy by taking a break.

Caring for yourself is not selfish. It helps make sure you can be your best you. If you want to be a good parent, employee, spouse, or friend, you have to first make time for yourself. You cannot give to others when your well is dry. Think about a small step you can take to make yourself a priority. One simple thing. That's it.

The idea that self-care has to be this lavish thing that costs a bunch of money and takes a ton of time is false. I think this was what first made me think there was no way I would have the time (or the funds) to participate in self-care. There was no way I was going to be able to take a week off from work and fly to an exotic island where I sipped cocktails out of a coconut. If I couldn't do that, why should I even bother? It was an easy out. An excuse I could get behind and continue on the path of self-sabotage and self-hatred.

The more I pushed back, the more I needed some self-care in my life. One day while I was visiting a client at the hospital, I remember passing a waiting room and wishing I was in there so I could have a few minutes to read a book or magazine. This was my wake-up call. I had wished for some ailment so I could have time for myself. I knew I needed to change how I was living my life.

At the time I was working full time and was my mother's part-time caregiver. I was also a full-time college student and had three children under the age of six. To top this off, I was living in a house full of domestic violence. I had no time for myself, not even in the bathroom. Every moment I had was consumed with something I had to do; my needs did not make the list. I was expected to make sure everyone else had what they needed, but I had nothing left to give.

In that moment, as I walked past a waiting room in a hospital, I knew I had to do something to change the path I was on. I took a good look at myself and how I was allowing myself to come last. The excuses crept in when I even thought about doing something for myself. The money could be better used for the kids. I should spend every free minute with my children. I shook these thoughts out of my mind and started small. I popped in my favorite Tom Petty CD into my car stereo and took the long way home. I took a walk alone and listened to the birds, which was enough to help me check in with myself and relax. A hot bubble bath with the bathroom door locked and music on to drown out the knocking on the door helped relieve tension and let me have a great night's sleep. A cup of tea and a good book helped take my mind off my worries long enough to quiet my mind. Simple, inexpensive activities helped me begin to take care of my needs and put myself back on my list of priorities.

When I had extra money, I scheduled a massage or a pedicure. I didn't feel guilty because I saw the impact these acts had on my overall life. The more I valued myself, the less I allowed others to take me for granted. The small steps helped me make changes in my life and things began to change.

I learned that self-care does not have to cost money or take a lot of time; it just has to honor you. Think about what you enjoy doing that you have not done in a while. Do you like to take hot bubble baths? How about going for a walk under the stars? Is there a special shampoo or body wash you love but you haven't bought? Do you enjoy a hot cup of tea? How about a good book or a funny movie? What is one thing you could do today to honor yourself?

Exercise:

Find at least one thing you are going to start doing for yourself. Pick something you will enjoy, not something that will add stress to your life. Open up your calendar and add the item to your schedule (and make sure your alarm is on!!). When the alarm goes off, make sure you take the time to do the activity you have chosen.

Examples of self-care activities:

- Take a hot bath
- Post inspiring notes around the house

- Listen to music
- Exercise
- Meditate
- Practice yoga
- Cook or bake
- Write a poem
- Read poetry
- Make a Pinterest board of inspiring quotes
- Take a nap
- Organize one area in your home
- Spend time in nature
- Take a walk
- Watch funny videos
- Go to a support group meeting
- Make a playlist of your favorite songs
- Read a book you've wanted to
- Watch a funny movie or show
- Listen to an audiobook
- Get Reiki
- Have a cup of coffee
- Write positive affirmations and recite them
- Drink more water
- Diffuse essential oils

To find a list of more self-care activities, go to www.jessicaaikenhall.com/selfcare.

Loving Your Inner Child

When I first heard about loving my inner child, I thought the concept was foolish. How would pretending my five-year-old self still existed help me? And why would I waste time talking to her? It took me a while to get on board with this idea. I remember my counselor asking me, "What would she need to feel loved?"

I had no idea, and honestly, I didn't know she existed. I had read about healing our inner child and didn't buy into it. It sounded too far out there to be real, and if by chance it was real, what good would really come from it? I brushed off her question and started talking about something else. She stopped me and asked again.

"I don't know." I shrugged my shoulders in annoyance that she wasn't going to drop it.

"Close your eyes and ask her."

I closed my eyes as she suggested and sat in the quiet of the room. I didn't want to play this game with her. I respected my counselor, but I didn't want to do what she was asking. It felt weird.

"Go ahead, ask her." The softness of my counselor's voice gave me enough sympathy to humor her.

"What do you need?" A tear ran down my cheek as the vulnerability of the moment allowed the little Jessica to come forward. "She needs to feel safe."

"Ask her what she needs to feel safe."

"What do you need to feel safe?" I waited for her to answer me. "She said she needs to know that I'll protect her, and that I won't leave her."

"Can you do that for her?"

"Yes." In my mind, I could see the younger version of myself come forward. I couldn't hold the emotion back anymore. That little girl was so hungry for love and acceptance, I couldn't deprive her of it any longer.

"I want you to tell her she did the best she could, and she did nothing to deserve the abuse she went through. Her parents were sick, it wasn't her fault." My counselor's voice pulled me out of my head long enough to hear her words.

"It wasn't your fault. You were a good girl. You didn't deserve to be hurt. I will keep you safe now."

"Is there anything else you'd like to tell her?"

"I love you. I won't leave you." When I opened my eyes, my heart felt lighter. I hadn't ever given the child me any credit, and I had never shown her love. When I could look at my younger self as a five-year-old child, I could see her pain and her fear. That little girl had been working so hard to be brave while she faced the world alone. I could see aspects of her in my life and I could see the why behind many of the challenges I had faced.

It was easy to reject and be harsh to the adult me, but to say those awful, hurtful things to a child seemed cruel. When I understood that when I was hard on myself, I was also being hard on the wounded child, it became easier for me to offer myself compassion.

Inner child work is powerful. It's a great tool to work on healing past trauma and uncovering your needs. Be gentle with yourself as you learn to love the little child that is trapped inside of you, waiting for your acceptance and love.

Self-affirmations

Self-affirmations are simple, positive statements that state specific goals you wish to attain. Although they can sound rather basic, they have profound effects on the conscious and unconscious mind. When you repeat the self-affirmations, you begin to reprogram your mind. They help you push out the negative thoughts and replace them with positive beliefs. Self-affirmations are more proof that words hold power.

The first time I tried to use self-affirmations, I felt silly. The thought that I was telling myself things that weren't true felt strange. I repeated the words I needed to believe, and soon I did. The self-affirmations chased out the negative thoughts and helped me change my way of thinking.

If using positive affirmations is new to you, expect to feel a little uncomfortable to start. The more you practice, the easier they will become. Pick self-affirmations that you are able to believe. When you believe what you say, this exercise will help build your self-esteem. Try not to pick ones that will cause you undue stress when you cannot achieve them.

Exercise:

Select a few self-affirmations and say them out loud in the morning and throughout your day. Write them down and leave them in places you will see them and remind yourself to recite them. Some good spots include the bathroom mirror, the dashboard in your car, and your bedroom

The list below includes some self-affirmations you can use or make up some that will work for you.

- I am freeing myself from doubt and fear.
- I accept myself for who I am.
- I am not my past.
- I do not compare myself to others.
- I choose to be happy.
- I can achieve anything I set my mind to.
- I allow myself to heal.
- I can do this.
- I will reach my goals.
- I am generous.
- I trust my intuition.
- I breathe in calmness and breathe out anxiety.
- I let go of anger.
- I refuse to give up.
- The answer is right before me.
- I am comfortable in my own skin.
- I am enough.
- I will no longer criticize myself.
- I am a good person.
- I approve of who I am.
- I will not give up.
- The past has no power over me.
- All that I need comes to me at the right time. I am not alone.
- I have the right to share my story.

Mantras

Mantras are similar to self-affirmations in the sense that they are positive sayings used to help build you up. Mantras are sayings used to help center you and are tools for your mind. When meditating or sitting quietly, repeating a mantra can help keep the negative thoughts at bay. Mantras can give you a focal point to bring you peace when you are feeling overwhelmed or stressed.

Examples of Mantras:

- I belong. I have faith.
- Love is in everything. Love is everything.
- I am full of light.
- Remember who you are.
- Everything happens right on time.
- Things are not done to me; they just happen.
- Nothing lasts forever. Not the good. Not the bad.
- Love the life you have.
- No one can take my joy.
- Tomorrow is a new day.
- Inhale. Exhale.
- I choose love.

Pick one or two from the list or write your own. Practice reciting the mantra of your choice as you meditate or when you're sitting quietly. Listen to the words that you are speaking and let them settle around you and let them replace your worry with peace.

Forgiveness

Forgiveness is a huge part of healing. When you're not ready to release your trauma, forgiveness is often out of reach. I have heard from many survivors that the person who caused them pain does not deserve to be forgiven. I've had this thought myself a time or two and the argument that always wins is the forgiveness is for you, not them. The first time I heard this I remember how angry it made me. How dare you tell me to forgive the man who almost killed me. I felt the rage multiply within me and the fury boil my blood. And then I saw. I was given a glimmer of hope into what life could be like with forgiveness and I was ready to give it a shot.

The piece that sold me on forgiving was that when I held onto the resentment, anger, hatred, spite (you get the idea), I'm the prisoner. I'm the one who is being punished. The hold they have over me intensifies. I might be merely a fleeting thought to the man who raped me, but my hatred for him consumed me. My anger linked me to him. I couldn't heal when I held onto the idea that I needed to make him pay for what he did to me. In contrast, I was the one paying repeatedly. The pain he caused me continued hurting me with every pang of anger I felt.

When I tried forgiveness, I noticed the effects right away. The heaviness I had held onto lifted. My rapist no longer roamed my thoughts. I was free. And just because I forgave him didn't mean what he did to me didn't matter and wasn't wrong. It just took my power from him and it was returned back to me. I wasn't forgiving him for him, but for me. Forgiveness is the best gift you can give yourself.

Are there people you need to forgive? Make a list of the people you still hold resentment toward. Your list may be small when you start out, but it may grow as you get deeper in your story. People you may have forgotten about may come to the surface and your list may grow. Take a moment to feel the anger or hurt and then with a deep breath release it.

When you work on forgiveness, don't forget the most important person to forgive—you! Most of us have years of things we need to offer ourselves forgiveness for. Offer yourself as much grace as you offer others.

Meditation

Meditation has been around for thousands of years and is known as a mind-body medicine. It offers many benefits, including relaxation, inner peace and stress reduction. During meditation, you begin to develop internal focus, which helps to minimize negative or intrusive thoughts.

Meditation can be a useful tool when you write your story. It can quiet your mind when your thoughts become too much. If it is a tool you find helpful, make it a part of your daily routine. There are many types of meditations. I list three examples below.

Meditation for Relaxation

If you're new to meditation, it's normal for thoughts to come in and distract you as you try to quiet and calm your mind. It's helpful to use imagery to focus on while meditating.

1. Create a clear mental image of something or someone you enjoy and find comfort in.

Some examples:
- A best friend's face
- A field of wildflowers
- Your bare feet on a sandy beach
- Your pet
- Your safe place

2. Take three deep breaths.

3. Use one of these examples or one of your own to focus your attention and then focus on meditating. If worries or negative thoughts keep entering, allow them to wander through your focus, noting them and allowing them to pass through without concentrating on them.

If focusing on an image does not work for you, try repeating a word or syllable (such as "peace" or "om").

Try this for five minutes at first. Work your way up to ten, and then fifteen minutes.

Body Scan Meditation

The body scan can be performed while lying down, sitting, or in other postures. The steps below are a guided meditation designed to be done while sitting.

- Begin by bringing your attention into your body.
- You can close your eyes if that's comfortable for you.

- You can notice your body seated wherever you're seated, feeling the weight of your body on the chair, on the floor.
- Take a few deep breaths.
- And as you take a deep breath, bring in more oxygen into the body. And as you exhale, have a sense of relaxing more deeply.
- You can notice your feet on the floor, notice the sensations of your feet touching the floor: the weight and pressure, vibration, heat.
- You can notice your legs against the chair, pressure, pulsing, heaviness, lightness.
- Notice your back against the chair.
- Bring your attention into your stomach area. If your stomach is tense or tight, let it soften. Take a breath.
- Notice your hands. Are your hands tense or tight? See if you can allow them to soften.
- Notice your arms. Feel any sensation in your arms. Let your shoulders be soft.
- Notice your neck and throat. Let them be soft. Relax.
- Soften your jaw. Let your face and facial muscles be soft.
- Then notice your whole body present. Take one more breath.
- Be aware of your whole body as best as you can. Take a breath. And then when you're ready, you can open your eyes.

Loving Kindness Meditation

Loving kindness meditation begins with a focus on the self and then on someone you love. Next, you shift your focus to someone you have had difficulties with and then end with a focus on all beings. When you feel ready, the "difficult person" could be the perpetrator of the trauma you experienced. But to start, choose a difficult person who is less triggering.

1. Begin in a comfortable seated position.
2. Close your eyes if you are comfortable doing so.
3. Place your hand on your heart and take a deep breath in and out.
4. Maintain your hand placement and deep breathing as you recite the following verses out loud or to yourself:

> May I be free from suffering.
> May I experience pure joy.
> May I be at peace.
> May (someone you love) be free from suffering.
> May (someone you love) be at peace.
> May (a person you have had difficult interactions with) be free from suffering.
> May (a person you have had

difficult interactions with) experience joy.
May (a person you have had difficult interactions with) be at peace.
May all beings be free from suffering.
May all beings experience pure joy.
May all beings be at peace.

If you'd like to find more types of meditations, you can search online. If you would like to try a guided meditation, YouTube has a lot of options. Find one you enjoy and give it a shot!

Experiencing difficult emotions:

When you start to remember events from your past, you'll most likely experience difficult emotions. These may be emotions you have pushed away for years, hoping that if you didn't give them your attention, they may just go away. Healing is hard work, and with it comes pain and sadness. Don't let these emotions push you off the path you're on. Embrace them and let yourself feel.

When you give yourself permission to feel all the emotions, you remain in control. Let the sadness wash over you, but remember you have the tools you need to pick yourself up after. In order to heal, you have to feel.

You cannot heal what you do not allow yourself to feel. Feeling sad isn't fun, and if you are not careful, the feeling can morph and grow into more intense emotional pain. Once you've allowed yourself to feel, there are ways to pull yourself out of the pain.

Ways to distract yourself when you are feeling sad/down/blue

Distract your body

- Splash water on your face or take a cold shower.
- Engage in intense exercise (like running or jumping) to expand your physical energy.
- Engage in deep breathing, counting each breath. When your mind wanders, start back at one.

Distract yourself with a different emotion

- Watch a brief comedy sketch.
- Watch a brief video that invokes positive emotion.
- Watch a scary movie.

Distract yourself with activities

- Organize a drawer in your house.

- Go for a walk.
- Call a friend.

Distract yourself with thoughts

- Pick up a book or magazine and read the words out loud, backward.
- Write out the lyrics to a favorite song.
- Do a crossword puzzle.

Distract yourself with kindness

- Write someone a thoughtful email or card.
- Make a food or gift bag and distribute it to someone in need.
- Do something thoughtful for a friend.

It's okay to feel every emotion as they come and it's also okay to use the tools you have to move on out of the pain. You do not have to stay in the sadness once you move through the memory. Use the power you have been gaining and claim your strength back. You are stronger than anything you have been through. You are in control now.

Be Gentle With Yourself

As you begin taking the steps for the P.O.W.E.R. method, be gentle with yourself. There is a lot of information to learn or revisit. Everyone learns at their own pace and not all of the concepts will work for everyone.

If something doesn't seem doable or helpful skip it. Find the tools that will work for you. Pick things you will actually do and don't beat yourself up if you can't do it all. Be gentle with yourself and give yourself credit for taking the first steps in reclaiming your power.

Power Hint: You have to love yourself at every stage of the way when you write your story.
Power Prompt: What do you love most about life?

4

Work on Answering Some Important Questions Before You Begin

"The scariest moment is always just before you start." ~**Stephen King**

Now that you've gotten the groundwork out of the way, it is time to answer some important questions before you write your first draft (which may be the only one you write). There is a lot that goes into a decision to share your story. It is worth your time to consider some things before you spend too much time writing, so you know what direction you will go in.

When I began writing my memoir, I considered nothing other than getting the words on the page. I knew I wanted to hold my book in my hand, but that was all I knew. I didn't know how to write a memoir or manuscript of any kind. I also didn't know what had been in my way stopping me from getting to the finished product (whatever that meant).

After I wrote the first draft of my memoir, I took time to answer some of these questions, but others I learned later would have been helpful to have considered during the process. I know it sounds like a lot of work, and maybe even a step you can skip, but trust me when I tell you, you'll be glad you took a pause. A little time now will save you a lot of time as you get further into the process.

Your Why

Your why for wanting to write your story might be one of the most important questions you ask yourself. It will guide you down the correct path and save you a ton of time. If the reason you want to write your story is to heal and you have no desire to share the finished product with anyone, feel free to take an enormous sigh of relief. This is as important as any of the reasons to write your story, but it will leave you with less work, and probably fewer restrictions. If your goal is to write your story to release the pain and the memories, all you have to do is write (and write and write). You will not need to worry about who will read what you write, you won't even need to be concerned with spelling or grammar. You will, however, still need to put your foundation in place and take care of yourself throughout the process. The process of reliving your trauma doesn't change. It might be the one way that exposes the most secrets. When you know no one else will read the words you write, you will allow yourself all the freedom in the world.

Do you want to leave your story behind for your family and friends? Do you want the work you put into your story to be something people in your family will pick up a hundred years from now and get to know you and understand the life you lived? Do you want your story to become your legacy? If this is the case, you will most likely leave some things out. You will have full control over what makes it into the story and what you leave out. Your audience will be small, but it will still be for your consideration. Are there events in your past that you really don't want your grandchild to know about? These are things you will need to think about as you begin to write your story.

Are you thinking about publishing your memoir so the entire world can read your story? This one will hold the most censorship. Not only will you want to consider what you share, but you will want to consider who you share about and what might come from that. Also, you will have a word count goal, if you self-publish this is less important, but still worth considering. When you put your story out into the world, you'll have to consider what other people will think. Is your skin thick enough to hear feedback from strangers? This should not hold you back but be a reminder of just how much you want to make public.

The good news is you can change your mind along the way. You can start out with the goal of using your writing to heal past trauma and end with a memoir in your hand. You can also start with the goal of publishing your memoir and end at a fire pit burning the story that caused you so much pain. You can also write your first draft to heal, write your second draft for your family, and then polish it a little more and publish your memoir. You are in control of your story now. It is up to you what you share, and what you leave out.

Why Haven't You Written Your Story Yet?

If you're like me, you've known you've wanted to write your story for a long time. Decades, maybe. So, why haven't you written it yet? We all have different reasons for not taking action (but look at you! You're here, taking a huge first step!) and turning our dream into a reality. For me I had an excuse at every corner. I didn't have time. I didn't have the equipment. I didn't have the knowledge. I didn't know how to start. I was scared.

Whatever your reason, it is valid. But it does not have to control you. Once you figure out what has been stopping you from writing your story, you can become aware when you begin to stall your progress. You are the only thing standing in your way now. If you really want it, you'll find a way to make it happen.

What's in Your Way?

So, you've made a commitment to turn off the excuses and start writing… but you still haven't started. Or you started, but there is something getting in your way to fulfill this dream of yours. What is it? What is standing in your way? Do you have unsupportive family members or friends that are not allowing you the time or space to get the words out? Are you finding yourself looking at your phone to get out of writing? Have you started bingeing a new favorite show? When you can pinpoint what is standing in your way, you will be able to address it, and be aware when it creeps back in.

Exercise:
My Biggest Distraction

What are your biggest distractions? What is keeping you from making time to write? What is getting in your way? What excuses are you making?

Examples of distractions: Social media, TV, my kids

- Get a piece of paper and write a list of your distractions.

Once you've completed your list, take some time to look it over. Be mindful of your distractions. Notice if you are letting your distractions get in your way. Taking breaks is healthy, but procrastination is a form of self-sabotage. *You deserve to tell your story*.

What Are You Most Afraid of?

When you think about writing your story, what are you most afraid of? Is the fear holding you back? When I began writing my memoir, the things that scared me the most was hurting someone I loved and not finishing it. As the memories flew from my fingertips to the computer screen, I would stop and consider how the person I was writing about would feel, or what people would think about me. An overwhelming sense of dread would always follow these thoughts as I imagined my manuscript hanging in the cyberworld and never making onto paper. When I could push these thoughts out of my mind, I was able to finish.

What is the one thing you are most afraid of? Take a few minutes to think about it and listen to the fear. Validate it, and see what you can do to address it. Maybe just the act of listening is all that needs to happen.

What Are You Most Excited About?

Now that you have gotten your fear out of the way, what are you most excited about when you think about telling your story? The answer to this question might help you determine your why for writing your story. When I was writing my memoir, the things I was most excited about, and the thing that kept me focused was being able to cross a huge item off my bucket list. It was a close second when I could hold my completed book in my hand. The joy both of these events brought me was worth every second of pain and hard work along the way.

Take a few minutes and think about what you are most excited about writing your story. I can see the smile spreading across your face. That. Harness that right there, and every time you doubt yourself, remember how good this feels. Whatever it is you desire, it is within your reach. Let the excitement grow and push your fear out.

This is what you are after. This is what is going to make it all worth it.

What Would Happen If You Didn't Share Your Story?

Now, think about what would happen if you listened to the fear, or you gave up. What would happen if you didn't share your story? How would it feel to keep these words and secrets locked inside of you? I can tell you that there are millions of people who die without ever sharing their story. There are people who take their last breath with a story stuck in their heart. I have sat next to them as I watched them transition from this world without ever telling anyone the secrets that have haunted them.

Think about the amount of stories that have left this earth because people were unable to share them. On the flip side of this, I have sat with people as they lay dying in their hospital bed, who used every last bit of breath they had to tell me their story, just so someone would know it. Some of these people could not let go until they could say what they needed to say.

What would be the worst thing that would happen if you did not share your story and release your secrets? Take a few minutes to think about it, and then answer this: would you be able to live with yourself? Or would you be filled with regret?

I knew I could not stop the urgency to share my story. I had to get the words out. I had to let go of the secrets they had programmed me to keep. There was no other option for me. Is there for you?

What kind of story do you want to write?

When you think about telling your story, what do you imagine? Do you picture yourself taking pages of writing to a fire pit and watching it burn? Letting all of your pain and sadness burn and turn to ash to be carried away with the wind? Or do you plan to keep the words that you write? And, if you do, what do you want to do with them?

Do you love writing in your journal and feel content leaving your story there? Are your secrets too close to your heart to share them yet? Do you want to keep your writing just for you? Maybe you don't want to share your writing until you pass away; it can be a gift your loved ones stumble upon when they are mourning your loss. If this sounds like the path you want to take, writing in your journal may be just what you need to do.

Do you want to keep a detailed account of your life from birth to the present moment? You might want to consider writing your autobiography. This is typically what people write to leave for their family. Readers rarely find ordinary people's lives interesting enough to want to read the span of their life in entirety. If your goal is to write your story to leave behind your legacy or share pieces of family history, an autobiography may be for you.

Do you want to write your story as essays? Short pieces of writing that covers specific times and events in your life? You have the ability to cover what you want while leaving out what you don't. These essays can be shared in publications or on your own blog and even turned into a book. If the word essay scares you, but the idea sounds intriguing, consider writing letters to create your story. The letters can be to people from your life, to yourself or even to your readers. These letters can also be turned into a book.

Do you have your heart set on writing your memoir? Do you want to share your story with the world? Do you dream about holding a physical copy of your book in your hand as you flip through the pages? We'll talk more about this in Chapter 8.

When you decide what kind of book you want to write, you will determine what your next steps will be. My suggestion is, even if you plan on sharing your story with others, use the first draft of your story as a place to let go of everything. Release every secret you have been holding onto and let the paper hold your pain. If there are pieces you do not want to share with anyone, now might be the perfect time to start up the fire. Even if it takes longer to get to your end goal, take the time to get the words out. This is where the true healing will come from.

Set Your Goals

If you're anything like me, having a goal will help you succeed. Start with a small goal, one that is attainable.

Make your goal as specific as possible. What will you do and for how long?

When you meet that goal, set a new one. And when you reach that one, set another. The idea is to get to the finish line. If you've wanted to tell your story for decades, imagine how good it will feel when you reach your goal. It is within your reach.

An example of a reachable goal: Write fifteen minutes Monday through Friday. Find the time in your schedule and add it to your calendar.

When you can reach this goal, set another. Write one chapter every week.

If you are feeling confident, it might be time to give your finished product an end date. If you notice you can commit to your smaller goals, you will be able to get a sense of when you might reach the finish line. Pick a date and add it to your calendar. Before you know it, you will be ready for the next step!

Exercise:

Set your first writing goal. Write it somewhere you'll be able to see it.

Once you've spent some time answering these important questions, you are ready to begin writing. Get yourself in the right frame of mind before you begin. When you are aware of your reasons for wanting to share your story and know what's been in your way, you hold the power to get the words out. If you start to struggle or even feel like giving up, remember your why. The reason you want to release your story. You have the tools, don't forget to use them.

Power Hint: Create writing habits. Write every day, start with fifteen minutes a day for twenty-one days to develop a habit.
Power Prompt: What scares you the most?

5

Explore Memories from Your Past

"You can't go back and change the beginning, but you can start where you are and change the ending." ~C. S. Lewis

As you think about sharing your story, you might feel overwhelmed. You probably have an idea of what you want to include, at least some of the pieces, but what about the rest? Your life has been filled with so many moments it's hard to know which ones to include and which ones to leave out. When you think back to your why, the reason you want to share your story, this question may be answered. If there is a specific period in your life you want to write about, you may already know the path you are going to take, but you may be filled with questions.

Where should you begin? What should you write? What shouldn't you write? How will you remember everything you want to include? The questions can easily spin out of control and make the process too intimidating to even start. The negative self-talk may creep in telling yourself you don't even have a story to tell. You'll probably hear this a lot, but remember how to exchange the negative words for positive ones, reminding yourself *you* have a story to tell.

When I started thinking about what I wanted to write about, it felt impossible to get my thoughts together. So much had happened that I knew I wanted to share, but there were other moments that I wanted to include that I couldn't quite remember. I needed to do some research and explore the parts of my past I had forgotten about.

Some tools I used included looking through old pictures, making a timeline, brainstorming and writing prompts. These tools, as well as some others that will help you explore your memories, are shared in this chapter. As with everything in this book, use only what will help you. If there is something suggested that you don't feel will help you or will add more stress to your life, skip it. Find what works for you and get the memories from inside your head and onto the paper (or computer screen)!

Use Photos

A photograph can take you on a journey back into your past. Looking at one picture can awaken memories you had not thought about in decades. Photos are a powerful way to get your memories flowing. Photos hold a lot of history. Pictures are captured moments, and they also help remind us of what was not captured.

Pick up a photo (or scroll through your digital

archive) and study it. What do you see? Obviously, what is in the picture, but what else? Can you close your eyes and bring that time back to life? Can you hear what was going on around you? Are there any smells that are coming back to you?

These memories are not forgotten, they just don't stay in our present consciousness until there is a nudge or reminder. I can find a picture from when I was six years old, and I am transported back in time. The emotions from the day are as fresh as the day they happened. I can remember what happened before the memory was captured, and what happened after. For a moment I am that six-year-old little girl again, and I can see the world through her eyes.

When you use photos, you may find pieces of your story you had forgotten about. It might also be helpful for you to remember who you were at the different stages of your life. When you can see your story through your eyes as a child, teenager, or young adult, you may find compassion for that younger version of *you*.

If you are looking to stir up memories, this is a great exercise for you. If your story is filled with pain, this might help you remember some of the better times. When you do an inventory of your life, it is helpful to remember the good, too. This helps balance things out. When there is only pain, hurt, sorrow and loss, it becomes overwhelming. Take some time to find some good memories, too.

Exercise:
Let's go on a photo journey!

Pick a photo and ask yourself these questions:
- What were you wearing?
- Who were you with?
- How old were you?
- What happened the day before? The day after?
- What sounds, smells, and emotions does this bring up?
- What else does this memory evoke?
- Describe the place where the photo was taken.
- Describe the other people in the photo and their relation to you.
- What happened right before this photo was taken? After?
- What surprises you about this picture, now that you really look at it?
- Who is missing from this picture? Why?
- What can't we see in the picture?
- If that person in the picture could talk, what would he or she be saying?

Ask Family Questions

If you are lucky enough to have family members available to ask questions to, by all means ask them! I am envious of the people who have this opportunity. Currently, my oldest living relative is my older brother, and he remembers less than I do, but it was helpful to talk some things over with him as I wrote my story. I used this as a sort of fact check when I wasn't sure of a memory or event.

It's helpful to understand situations from other people's perspectives. What they remember about a situation might differ totally from what you do. Keep in mind that everyone sees the world through their own eyes, and just because they remember something differently than you do does not mean you are wrong (or they are, either). This just means you had different experiences.

Some questions to ask your family:

- Where was I born?
- What time was I born?
- What was your pregnancy like?
- What was the birth like? Were there any complications? Who was there?
- How did you feel when you saw and held me for the first time?
- What were your expectations for my life?
- Were there any foods I loved or hated?
- Who did I play with?
- What was my favorite toy?
- What was my first word?
- How did I react when my brothers or sisters were born?
- How did they react to me?
- How old was I when I took my first steps?

- Who was the first best friend I brought home?
- Who was my first boyfriend/girlfriend?
- What did you think of him/her?
- What did I say I wanted to be when I grew up?

If you do not have family members to ask these questions to, you will still be able to write your story. I didn't have anyone to talk with as I wrote my memoir, but I could piece my memories together from the stories I had been told as a child as well as photos I had found.

Some other ways that could be helpful to connect some of the missing dots is to look at old newspapers or documents online. Since writing my memoir I began researching my ancestry and have found so much out about family members I had never met. You may have to get creative if there is no one to ask, or you may have to rely on your memory. As long as you are honest and tell your truth, your healing will happen. Details do not have to be important. If there is something you don't remember, you can leave it out, or you can just write that you are unsure. *You are in control of your story.*

Make a Timeline

When I started writing my memoir, I wrote a quick list of everything I wanted to include. As I studied the list, I was confused about when certain events happened when it was in that form. I continued writing without being fully sure of the time sequence and ended up stuck. I stumbled over memories. I was sure I knew the order of events; it was my life after all, but I was wrong. After a few thousand words, everything felt like a tangled ball of yarn. I had a hard time wrapping my head around when events fit together. In one section I wrote about my dad's death and then wrote about him still being alive a few pages later.

When the mess was too much to fumble through, I had to stop and create a timeline. It seemed like a waste of time at first, and probably why I ended up in the mess I was in, but it ended up saving me hours of time trying to figure out how everything fit together. I took my list and fit the events onto my timeline and could see the order of the events I wanted to include.

Timelines are such a helpful tool when writing your story. They can help organize events, memories, and even emotions. To create a timeline it is helpful to have a piece of paper for every decade, so if you are forty-five you would have five sheets (0-10, 11-20, 21-30, 31-40 and 41-45). On each sheet of paper draw a line across the middle and then add smaller lines off this line, one for each age. Once you have every page filled out, write every pivotal moment in your life that you remember. When you are finished with this, go back through and add anything else you feel is important. Go back through a third time and add all the people who were significant. For me, I would add my dad's death when I was ten and my gram's death when I was twenty-seven. You can go back through another time and add any emotions you felt during an event or situation. For me, when I went to my first Tom Petty concert, I would add excitement and when I left my abusive partner, I would add fear.

It might be helpful to use different colors to help stay organized. If you are more artistic, you can draw the events on your timeline and use a key to keep track of things. The goal is to make your timeline work for you. This is a document you can go back to and add things as you remember them.

You also do not have to start at the beginning. You can start wherever you want to start. If you remember little of your childhood, or it's a period you do not want to address, you can skip to the age you are comfortable with. When you're finished with your timeline, it is helpful to go over it and look for patterns, connections, and a-ha moments. Often there are things that happen repeatedly in our lives and when we have the chance to look at the whole picture, it can help put things into perspective. When I created my timeline, I noticed there were multiple instances of domestic violence, abuse and loss, but also of hope, love, and friendships. This look back can help you determine the theme of your story (if you plan on using your story to create a memoir).

Sample timeline:

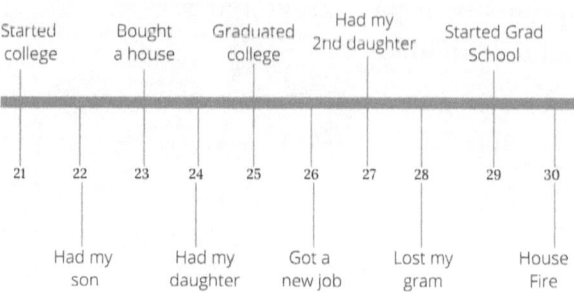

Ideas of what to include on your timeline:

- Birth
- Adoption
- Learning to ride a bike
- Puberty
- Getting your driver's license
- First kiss
- First time having sex
- Coming out
- First independent trip away from family
- Graduation
- Pregnancy
- Miscarriage/infertility/

- Pregnancy loss/stillbirth
- Childbirth
- Parenthood
- Marriage/partnership
- Wedding
- Midlife crisis
- Empty nest
- Death of a loved one
- Funerals
- Grieving process
- Menopause
- Divorce
- Leaving a loved one
- Committing to a career
- Switching careers
- Leaving your hometown
- Moving to a new town
- Travel
- Getting sober
- Retirement
- A spiritual awakening
- Extreme loneliness
- Secrets revealed
- Being a foster child
- Caregiving for an elderly parent
- Betrayal
- Incarceration
- Estrangement
- Making peace
- Chronic illness

- Mental illness
- Cancer
- A transformative diagnosis
- Diagnosed with PTSD or Complex PTSD
- Abuse survivor
- Traumas
- Addiction
- Being homeless
- Falling in love
- Pets
- Meeting a hero

Seventy-Seven Moments

A great way to get your ideas flowing and your memories working is to just write. Writing without a direction is helpful at times, but if you feel stuck and you're not sure what direction you should go in, try the exercise below. This is sort of like brainstorming, but you are working on a specific request. Write as many moments from your life as you can remember. Don't put too much thought into it, just move your pen across the piece of paper. Moments you may have forgotten about may come back to you and might spark more memories. The more you remember, the more you have to hang on to. The moments can be anything from something you considered being monumental to something trivial. Just get the words out of your head and onto the paper!

Exercise:

1. Number sheets of paper 1-77.
2. Set a timer for twenty minutes.
3. Write as many moments as you can remember. Don't think about it, just write.

Example:

1. My gram's soup
2. Traveling to Canada
3. Learning to drive
4. Going to NYC to see Tom Petty
5. Graduating college

When your list is complete, use it to help you remember what you want to include in your story. This is a great exercise to get your pen (or fingers) moving!

Brainstorm

Brainstorming is a great tool to help you remember events you want to include in your story. This is helpful to use when you work on your outline in the next chapter. Grab a piece of paper and a pen (or your computer) and just write everything that comes to mind. There is no need for organization, just let what comes. If you want to get a big piece of paper and some colored pens or markers, you can have some fun with this. For me, when I use my hands to write, I use a different part of my brain than when I type. Ideas and memories come to the surface easier this way for me. The idea is to get as much out of your brain as possible. You may not use the information for anything else, but it is fun to see what comes out!

What do you want to include?

After you have made your timeline, brainstormed and completed the seventy-seven moments exercise, go through them and make a list or use a highlighter and highlight what you want to write about. You can write about it all, or you can choose what you want to focus on. You can add to this list at any time, just as you can decide not to include things. This will work as your guide as you begin to write. If you get stuck or don't know what to write about, come back to this list and pick something.

Writing Prompts

You've done all the above suggestions, or at least the ones you felt were helpful, but you still don't feel ready to start writing. Maybe fear is holding you back, or you might just not know how to start. First, know you're not alone. Getting started can be the hardest part, but even after you've started, continuing the creative flow can be just as difficult.

To help jumpstart your creativity, try using writing prompts. Pick one related to your story, or one that has nothing to do with what you're writing about. The idea is to get your fingers (or pen) moving.

Want to give it a shot? Pick a writing prompt from the

list below or use one of the power prompts and get writing!

- How many life goals have you attained?
- What regrets do you have?
- What do you think the future holds for you?
- Do you spend more time planning for the future or living in the moment?
- What will your retirement be like?
- What will your obituary say about you?
- What did you do today?
- What is your favorite way to spend the day?
- What is your daily routine?
- What are three things you can't go without?

Once you picked one you want to try, write it out on the top of the page and set a timer for fifteen minutes and write. If nothing comes, rewrite the prompt and start again. You want to keep writing for the entire time, even if you write, "I have nothing to write. This is so dumb. I can't believe she thought this was a good idea."

As you are writing, even in protest the words will start to flow. Trust me!

Our lives are made up of many moments and memories. Some of them are harder to relive than others, and some leave you with a smile. Make sure you focus your attention on both. As you work to heal your trauma and take the steps to reclaim your power, don't forget to take time to cherish the memories and people who have given you joy.

Once you have had time to examine your past, take some time before you write your story to make sure you have what you need to stay safe and are taking the steps to take care of yourself. Your safety and self-care are critical steps along this journey. Don't skimp on them. You're worth it.

Now that you have some ideas of what you want to write, and you have the tools to get the words flowing… it's time to get started turning your memories into your story.

Power Hints:

- When you write your story, you get to control the story. You are in charge of what you share and what you leave out.
- Don't let the big picture overwhelm you. Start with one story at a time.
- Your life doesn't have to be an open book. You have the power to leave anything you want out.
- It's not what's wrong with you, but what happened to you.
- Keep a notebook and pen with you at all times; you never know when an idea will come, and you don't want to forget it.
- Be patient, be reflective, be humble, be

teachable, and be open to what the process might reveal to you.
- Take breaks, listen to your body. Most importantly, have fun!

Power Prompt: What reoccurring nightmares or dreams have you had?

6
Release Your Secrets and Turn Your Memories into Stories

"When you recognize and acknowledge your personal power, you no longer need to feel superior or inferior to anyone else." ~Deepak Chopra, M.D.

Now that you did the work in the previous steps and got some of your memories out, it's time to start writing. This is probably the hardest step, although it's self-explanatory; just write, it is way more involved than that. This is most likely the place you've been to before and you stopped before you even started because it feels overwhelming. You may even have written some before it became too much. Either way, this time will be different. You have the tools you need to keep going this time.

I know what it's like to want something so bad and not be able to achieve it. I've been there, and I've been where you are, too. I know how hard this step in the process is, but I also know how rewarding it is. Listen to your body and your heart as you work toward your goal. Take breaks if you need them, set your story aside and go back to the previous steps.

Make it a habit to take care of yourself every day. Put a self-care activity on your calendar and take the time to follow through with it. Have a cup of tea next to you as you write. Push out the negative self-talk when it takes over. Recite your mantras each day to help remind yourself how capable you are. You have all you need inside of you. You're on your way to finding yourself again and reclaiming your power.

Don't get discouraged with the process when it gets hard. There will be days that are harder than others and there will be days you'll have fun. The words will come some days and other days you might stare at a blank computer screen. When I started writing my story, I didn't know what to expect. I didn't think it was going to be as hard as it was or bring as much pain back to the surface as it did. Some days I couldn't write at all, even when I had planned to because it was too hard to go back to the pain. Even with taking days off and allowing myself time to reflect and heal, I still finished my story. I know you will be able to, too. Don't be hard on yourself. You will get to the finish line. Take it one memory at a time.

Trauma and Memory

As you try to pull up memories from your past, you

may become frustrated when they don't come. When you have experienced trauma, chances are you may have forgotten some events from your past. You also may remember things differently than other people who were there. This is normal. It is your brain's way of protecting you.

When I was writing my memoir, I tried to recall details from an incident that happened when I was six years old. I began writing about the time my mom tried to leave my dad. My fingers glided across the keyboard as the story poured out. And then they stopped. I closed my eyes to pull it up, but nothing would come.

I remember parts of that day like it happened yesterday. The fear I felt as I watched my dad break the window in the door and his hand come in through the broken glass radiated throughout my body. Tears streamed down my face as I saw my little body huddled together in a pile on the kitchen floor with my mom and older brother. Then the memories stopped. I can't tell you what happened next. It's easy to assume my dad got in and most likely caused extensive harm to us, but I can't remember.

I felt like a failure when the words wouldn't come. If I couldn't remember what happened, who's saying I even knew any of my story? I know it sounds silly, but I truly questioned everything. How could I forget something so significant? The entire event left me wondering about everything I thought I knew. Until that time, I didn't know I couldn't remember, and then I wondered what else I couldn't remember.

That question made me feel like a stranger inside of myself. How could I have lived this life and not even remember events that happened? I expected there would be things that wouldn't be clear, but I didn't expect incidents to be completely unavailable. This was a first for me and it left me with a feeling I did not like.

I talked with my counselor about this, and she explained to me it was normal. *Normal.* How in the world could it be normal to forget pieces of your own life? She told me it was my brain's way of protecting me. It was a coping mechanism that allowed me to shut out some of the most awful parts of my life so they couldn't cause me any more harm.

How awful did it have to be to have zero recollection? Bad enough. That's all. It just had to be bad enough for your brain to shut it out and let you move on. I considered working on remembering this event, but I didn't know what it would have done for me. There was a reason that event didn't have a place in my memory bank. I listened to my body and moved on without uncovering the rest of the story. By this time my mom had passed away and I didn't want to re-traumatize my brother by asking him what happened. I had to be okay with moving on without knowing.

As I progressed with my story, I stumbled on more events I couldn't remember. I wasn't as taken aback by them when I understood why. I was grateful for the protection. I knew there was something bigger than myself keeping me safe all those years. I just didn't know I was part of it.

For the same reason, you may remember things differently than they actually happened. Just as our brain keeps memories away from us, it also alters the way we remember things. This happens for the same reason. The best example I have for this is after someone in your life dies, you tend to remember only the good parts of that person and the relationship. You hold on to the good and let go of the bad. Our memory does the same. It's the way you can face all the things you have been through.

Even though you may not remember everything, or you remember things differently does not mean you are lying. It does not mean what happened to you doesn't matter. This is just how you have been able to cope with all you have been through. Don't be alarmed if some of your memories don't come. Also, I would suggest that you don't attempt to pull the memories back on your own. If you feel obligated to dig to find the truth, please make sure you are with someone who is trained to help you through the process. The memories have been suppressed for a reason. This is not something you should do on your own. Take care of yourself and honor the precautions that have been put in place to keep you safe.

Truth

When you write your story, it's important to tell the truth. If you want to write a memoir, it needs to be true or it cannot be considered a memoir. If you're writing to heal writing anything other than the truth will not help with your healing. Like the saying goes, the truth will set you free.

Since trauma can play tricks with your memory, it may have you worried about being able to tell the truth. Let me put your mind at ease—as long as you tell your truth, from your perspective you are telling the truth. It doesn't matter that someone else remembers it differently. All that matters is that you are coming from a place of truth.

Every one of us will remember events differently. There will be similarities, but it will not be one hundred percent the same. This is because everything we experience is personal to you and only you. I remember the day my dad died much differently than my brother remembers it. That does not change my reality, or his.

When my younger sister read my memoir, she was upset with me for how I portrayed our mother. She told me she thought I was lying about some events that were mentioned in my book. When we talked about this and I told her why I had written what I had, she seemed to understand I was telling the truth. There is a seven-year age difference between us, so there was a big part of my life she didn't exist. The mother I wrote about in my memoir was not the mother she knew, but she was the mother that raised me.

Even some events that took place after her birth she remembered differently than I had written about. When she put herself in my shoes, she could see I was telling my truth. My mother and sister had a much different relationship than my mother had with me. Although we lived in the same house, our experiences were very different.

There is a chance someone will question your memories, but their questioning does not mean you are not telling the truth. As long as you write what you remember as the truth, you do not have to prove anything to anyone else. You will write your best story when it comes from your heart.

Just Write

The best advice I can offer is just write. When you give yourself the freedom to write, anything can happen. Words you didn't know where lodged inside of you will come out. Memories will come to the surface that you had forgotten about. When you let your fingers glide across the keyboard or the pen across the paper, magic happens.

Even if you plan to write a memoir of your own, I still suggest you just write. Write without a plan. Write to get every single word out of your head. Write until you cannot write any more. If your goal is to release your story to heal, then you will want everything out in the open. Just because it is written does not mean you have to share it with anyone. You can write pieces that no one else will ever read. You can toss pages into the fire once you are done, but get it all out.

A friend once told me, "Let the paper hold it." When you let the paper hold your pain, you no longer have to bear its burden. You can release the pain and be free from the weight of carrying the secret. Watch the paper absorb the hurt and heartache as you fill it with words.

If you try too hard to write perfectly or beautifully, you may run into a wall. The words may not come if you are asking more from them than they can give you. Have no expectations when you first write. Just write.

Turn off your inner critic as you're writing. It's easier said than done, I'm well aware, but give it a shot. Every time you criticize your work, remind yourself you're doing the best that you can. Not only are you writing, but you are also healing. You are working through years of memories, heartache, and pain. The process might not be pretty, and that's okay. You'll have time to fix anything you find unsatisfactory later. Your job right now is just to get the words out.

Don't overthink what you are going to write and don't try to get it perfect. At this stage perfection is not something to strive for, it will slow you down and dry up your creativity. If you get stuck in a section, skip to another section. If you're not sure where to start, just write what comes to you. You can move things around later. Try not to put too much pressure on yourself. The more freedom you can give yourself, the easier the words will flow.

The best advice I can give you is don't look back. Don't take time to read what you've already written. Don't change words as you write. If you get stuck, make a note (you can write something like **come back to this later**) in bold so you'll be able to find it when you go back through to edit.

When I was writing my memoir, I could spend a full day reading through what I had already written. I spent an entire day I could have been writing, looking for the right word to make a section better than it was. It wasn't something that was even necessary, especially at that time in the process. I second guessed everything and let my critical voice take over. When I listened to my own advice and didn't go back through my writing before I was done, the words just flowed. Learn from my mistakes and just write.

Critical Voice

Your critical voice will try to stop you before you even get started, and then will try to keep stopping you. Just like with self-talk, you will need to turn your critical voice off as you write. It will sneak up on you when you least expect it, and it will make you want to quit. Don't let it win.

When I was writing my memoir (and every other book), my inner critic works overtime to try to talk me out of writing. To be honest, it has won a few times and stolen my creativity from me. Some things my critical voice has said to me:

- You don't know how to write.
- Who cares about your story, anyway?
- What's the point? No one's going to read it, anyway.
- Maybe I'm making this up. It didn't happen that way.
- This is awful. You call yourself a writer? (Insert judgmental laughter)
- This is boring.
- My family is going to be mad at me for writing this.

- What I went through wasn't that bad, others have been through much worse.

It's no wonder these words knocked me down a time or two. The mistake I made was listening to the words. They were *my* words, and I was letting them destroy me. This is a form of negative self-talk. In order to shut your inner critic up, remind yourself you have a story to tell. Try not to let your critical voice take away your voice. Know it will rear its ugly head and be prepared. Knowledge is power, and you own the power. Don't forget that and keep on writing.

What if you don't want to write?

Maybe you're not a writer. There could be many reasons that writing isn't for you. You can still share your story. There are ways around writing tons of words to reach the goal of finding your voice and healing trauma. If you want to write, just not that much you could consider starting a blog. You can write a short post, just long enough to get what you need to say out. This makes your story accessible to others, but if you don't advertise your blog, chances are you won't have a huge audience right away.

If writing even a little isn't your thing, you could consider using pictures to tell your story. If you use pictures, you can still include pieces of your story. One woman I worked with did this. She turned her story into a scrapbook and made copies for her family members. Her primary goal was to leave her legacy for her family.

If you're not camera shy, you could consider using a video camera to capture your story. This is also something you could leave for your family. Another option is voice recording your story. There are a few options for this. One is as simple as a tape recorder. You can talk your story into the device and leave it for loved ones or hire someone to transcribe it for you. Or you could use a dictation program such as Dragon Naturally Speaking that can turn your voice into a document.

Don't give up on your dream of getting the words out because you don't like to write. There are enough options out there that can accommodate your needs and desires. If you have the financial ability, you could also hire a ghostwriter. This is someone you would meet with and they would write your story for you. This can cost a lot of money, but if you hope to write your book and you do not want to, this is an option that might work for you.

Don't Forget the Good

When I was writing my memoir, all the memories that flooded me were overwhelming. The list of negative events grew every time I sat at my desk. There were so many things that had happened that I felt needed to be included in my story. At first I didn't write down any of the positive things that had happened. I was under the impression readers didn't want to know about that. I was wrong.

Readers want to get to know you. They want to see the struggles and learn what you did to overcome them, but they also want to see the good. Real life is made up of the good and the bad. You should include both to offer a well-rounded story. Readers are rooting for you. They would be disappointed if all they read was how awful your life was. It's important to let them see all aspects of your life.

It's easy to focus on the bad and only remember the trauma. Our lives are made up of many things and many memories. When we push away the positive, it leaves room for the negative to take its place. Dig deep if you need to.

Exercise:
Make a list of at least ten positive or happy memories. It doesn't matter how big or small they are!
1.
2.
3.
4.
5.
6.
7.
8.
9.
10.

When you start to feel overwhelmed with remembering the trauma or the bad memories, come back to this list for a reminder that there were good times, too.

Writing a life story filled with pain can be exhausting. Take your time and don't push yourself through the process. If the words come, let them out and release them. If a section is too hard to go back to, skip it and move onto something else. You control your story now and you are in control of what is shared and what you leave out. Make your main priority getting your words out in the gentlest way possible. Chapter seven has some helpful ideas to write through the painful memories.

Take care of yourself through the process. Take breaks when you need them. Practice self-care and take it one word at a time. You can do this. I know you can.

Power Hints:

- This is your story. It is not the place to tell someone else's story.
- Don't worry about being perfect—just get the words out. You can fix it later.
- You don't need to be a skilled writer—you just have to be willing.
- Don't go back and edit or read it. Write and move on—uncensored.
- If you don't enjoy writing, talk it out and have it transcribed.
- Try writing your story as the person the event happened to. Become *that* you again.

- Keep *you* in your story. Your voice is important. Don't hold back who you are.

Power Prompt: Choose one of your earliest memories and write about the event. Describe everything you can remember, including who was with you, what happened, your feelings, sounds, and smells.

7
How to Write Through the Pain

"Although the world is full of suffering, it is full also with the overcoming of it." ~Helen Keller

As you write your story, you may come across sections that are too painful to write. If this is the case, there are a few options to help you get your story out. The first option you have is to skip it entirely. This may not be the best choice, especially if your goal is to unload all of your secrets to release your trauma. If you decide you must write the section, there are some tricks to help get the words out.

When I was writing my memoir, there were a few sections I had to skip until the end. They were times in my life that had caused me the most pain and the most shame. I remember thinking how great it would have been to know what I know now then so I could have avoided so many hard lessons. That wasn't a possibility, and the wish was enough to intensify the uncomfortable feelings.

There were sections of my story I wrote as tears streamed down my cheeks, and others where I couldn't keep in the laughter. One of the hardest parts for me to write was about being put in foster care. During that time, I lost who I was. The pain from being tossed out of my family was overwhelming, and facing the memory made my stomach drop. If that moment of my life hadn't happened life as I know it today would have been completely different. I would have had more opportunities to either thrive or fail.

As I replayed the events in my mind, I took myself on an imaginary journey. I closed my eyes and watched the scene unfold differently. I was my fourteen-year-old self, and I saw my stepfather hit me and instead of fighting back, I went to my room and closed the door. I imagined life went back to normal and fantasized about what could have happened. I pictured myself at home with a happy family. I saw myself go off to college and meet new friends. I watched my entire life from that moment change, every opportunity open up and saw my life how it could have been.

I knew this was in fact a fantasy, and had I stayed in my abusive home, things would not have worked out how I imagined them. It was easy to picture a loving family and a simple life, but realistically I knew one change would not have altered much at all. I eventually would have gone into foster care, or maybe worse, been murdered by my stepfather. The thing is, when I tried to change how it could have been, I knew it was make believe. Just because I wanted it to happen differently, even if I had done something different, I wasn't the only one involved. If I had altered my actions, there is nothing to say the other people involved would have changed theirs.

The daydream of the perfect life was nice in the moment, but I knew it was not real. I also knew that had one thing changed, my entire life as I know it would be different. The good things I experienced, the people I met, the healing and growth I had worked so hard for would not exist. One change could have affected everything. When I could see the situation for what it was and where it brought me, I was able to face it.

The tears still came, and my heart was still heavy, but I could feel myself in my body, in my life as I know it and be present. I felt my fingertips hit the keys on the keyboard and watched words appear on the screen. I let the pain come and knew it could take nothing more from me. The scared teenager was no longer who I was, but I could honor where she had been.

I found some tools that helped me move through the process a little easier. I used character sketches and turned the people who had caused me pain into characters in my story. I changed their names, so they became strangers and not people I had loved. It seemed to hurt a little less when someone I didn't know inflicted pain on me.

I also wrote letters to the people from my past, including my past self. Some letters I wrote as requested by my counselor and others came when the pain was too much to bear. Some letters I watched burn as I sobbed. I was able to say what I had never been able to, and even after the recipient of the letters had died, I felt I was able to return the pain to them that they made me hold. I no longer had room for their abuse or control. When the words turned to ashes, I felt the pieces of me they had stolen return.

The tools I used were helpful for me, but they may not work for you. Give them a shot and see what will work for you. Sometimes the most painful experiences can bring the most healing. Give yourself plenty of time as you work through them. When you are working through these hard times, it is normal to experience body aches and fatigue. Take naps if your body is asking for rest, go for a walk to get fresh air, take a hot bath, and relax. Listen to your needs and be gentle with yourself.

Character Sketches

Have you ever thought of yourself as a character? I'm sure there are plenty of characters in your life! Using character sketches is a great way to distance yourself from the 'characters' in your story. When you turn people from your past into a character, they lose some of their power.

Your story will be made up of major characters, who occupy much of your story and minor characters who will take up less of the story. Take some time and make a list of the characters you want to include in your story. Make note if they will be a major or minor character. Don't forget to include yourself, you're the main character!

Exercise:

Character Sketch

On a sheet of paper write the following for each character and then complete the information:

Character name:
Main impression I want to convey:
Character's personality:
What the character says:
Character's physical appearance:
Anything else I want to include:

After you fill out a character sketch for each of the characters in your book, you can go back to it from time to time to make sure you have portrayed the character how you intended. This is a helpful exercise to turn the real people in your life into characters. When you take their power away from them, it is easier to write your story. Character sketches can help you view the people in your story as characters. You are in control of maneuvering these characters around in your story and what is shared about them. If a character had caused you pain in your life you might find it empowering to be in control of what you share about them.

Exercise:

How do you think people see you?

Take a minute and complete a character sketch for

you, as though you are a stranger. What do you want people to know about you? How do you want to be perceived? What is important for readers to know about you?

Write it As Letters

Another way to help write through difficult areas of your story is to turn the story into a letter to a specific person. There are endless ways to go about this, some examples are listed on the following pages. The most important piece to remember is you do not need to share these letters with anyone. They can be used specifically to help you move through an area in your story, or you can decide to use letters to write your book in its entirety. The choice is yours.

As I worked through some of the issues with my mom, dad and stepfather, it was suggested that I write letters to each of them by my counselor. She told me to write a letter explaining everything I wanted to say to them that I had never had the chance to tell them before. My mom and stepfather were alive when I wrote their letters, but I never intended on sharing what I wrote with them, they were strictly for my healing. I remember when I received the assignment, I didn't feel much of anything, except annoyed at having one more thing added to my to-do list. I figured it wouldn't do much good, and it was going to be a waste of my time. Just another one of those new age tricks counselors make their clients do.

I started with the letter to my dad. He had been dead

for over twenty years when I wrote the letter and figured it would be easy. I didn't think I had too much to say to someone I only knew for five years. He hadn't come into my life until I was three, and then when my parents split up, I only saw him for about fifty-two days a year. In the short time we had together, I figured he hadn't done enough to matter. Surely it wasn't enough to have caused me any trauma I needed to work through. When I sat down with a notebook and a pen, I soon learned how wrong I was.

Dear Dad, was followed by a mix of emotions. Questions about what life would have been like had he still been alive came and were followed by memories I had hidden for over twenty years. Memories of some of the worst abuse of my life. Memories of watching my father almost kill my brother. The sound of his violent rage echoed in my mind as I turned into the scared three-year-old little girl who wet the bed.

More memories came as my pen sped across the page. I turned the page and kept writing and writing and writing to a man I didn't think I knew. Tears from sadness and rage mixed together as they pooled in my eyes. How could I have forgotten so much of this? How could he have been just some man who made up half of my DNA? How could I have forgotten so much about him and about the time we did spend together?

When I finished the six-page letter, I held the pages in my hands and felt connected to a part of myself I hadn't known before. I uncovered trauma I had forgotten about, but found a better understanding of some events in my life that hadn't made sense. I felt closer to the man who was partially responsible for my existence.

The powerfulness of the exercise continued when I wrote letters to the people who were still living, the people who had been with me most of my life. I stared with a letter to my stepfather, because although he had caused me a lot of pain, I knew the letter would be shorter to him than to my mom. I poured my heart onto the paper and felt vulnerable as memories fell around me. I spoke for the seven-year-old girl he had molested and as the woman I became. I told him how confusing it was to be loved by someone who had caused me so much pain. I let him know how much he had stolen from me and how I wouldn't give him any more power over me or my life.

When it came time to write the letter to my mom, I was overcome with the most emotion. I had spent my life wanting her to love me and had always teetered on the edge to do whatever I could to make her see me. For the first time in my life, I put the words I had hung onto for so long in an attempt to protect her. As the words came, so did the anger. I didn't know how much she had hurt me until I watched the pages fill with pain. I wrote through the tears, not able to stop until I got every word out. When I burned her letter, I felt lighter. I felt free from years of neglect and never being good enough.

When I talked with my counselor after this exercise, I told her about my experiences. She suggested since I had such a reaction to the letter I wrote to my mom I should write her another one. She said there was more I needed to say. I didn't know how that could be true. I spent so much time getting every word out I didn't know how there could be anything left, but she was right. The next letter I wrote came from a different place. The anger had lifted, and I was able to write from a place of understanding. I wrote it knowing she herself was sick, and the things she had done to me were because of her illness. I wrote the next letter to the broken pieces of my mother. When I was finished with this letter, I felt my heart open. I knew I had forgiven her. My imprisonment from her spell had lifted.

With every letter I wrote, I could see my story from a different perspective. The letters gave me an opportunity to say what I needed to say, even if no one else would ever be able to read them. The letters helped me gather the strength I needed to tell the story I needed to tell.

Think about the people from your past. Is there anyone you need to tell something? Something you cannot speak? Try writing a letter. Use the letter as a place to let everything out. Don't hold anything back. Let the person know how much they hurt you or tell them how much they helped you. Not every letter needs to be addressed to a person who caused you pain. There are people in our lives who we would like to thank, use this as a tool for both. Writing letters is a great place to begin as you work through the pain. It will help you understand people and your reaction to them.

Another option is to write your entire story as a series of letters. This may take some of the freedom to write whatever you want away, but it could be a creative way to craft your book. You could have a section for each person, or each period of your life. The possibilities are endless. This could also be something you work on in your journal. Use this tool to help move you along either in the healing or the writing process, or both.

Do you want to write your story as a series of letters? It can be healing to write letters to the people who have hurt us or even helped us along our journey. Sometimes the only way to get it all out is to write it in a letter.

Below are some suggestions of letters to write:

- Letters to the people who hurt you- Write a letter to the people who hurt you. Tell them everything you want to say. Hold nothing back.
- Letters to the people you have unfinished emotional business with- Be candid in your letter, describing what your feelings are and what you need to say to the person.
- Forgiveness letters- Write a letter to each person you need to forgive. Tell them what you need to forgive and why. Write letters to the people you have wronged and need to ask forgiveness.
- Gratitude letters- Write a letter to someone you appreciate, someone who made a difference in your life. Include specific things this person has done for you and how he/she made you feel.
- A letter to your younger self from you today- Write a letter to your younger self -the you who went through the trauma. What would

- you say to comfort him/her? What advice do you have to offer? Offer your past self-acceptance, validations, and love.
- Write a letter to the person or event that hurt you- Then write back a response from this person or event.

Are there letters you want to write that aren't on the list? Give it some thought and make a list of the letters you want to write. Start with the one you are excited to write, either to get to the root of your pain, or to someone you love. You could write a version to keep and one to share. Writing letters to the people who have hurt you opens you up to deeper healing. Take it one letter at a time.

Try Writing in the Third Person

When you write your story, you will use the first person. You are the narrator and will use I, me and my. This can be especially hard when you are writing about past trauma. As you write in first person you are reliving the events, often causing pain and heartache along the way. If you come to a section that is just too hard to write, consider switching to third person. Let "someone" else be the narrator. You can use your name and the pronouns of your choosing. Jessica is using her experience to help you find ways to share your story. She learned the hard way and wants to make sure others know the tricks that helped get her to the finish line.

Writing in third person can help put a distance

between you and your story. It's easier to write about Jessica being placed in foster care than it is to write the painful details of the time I was taken out of my home when I was fourteen. It helps lessen the emotion attached to the event or memory. If your plan is to write your memoir you can start by writing the painful event in third person, and when you go back to work on your next draft, you can change it to the first person.

Give it a shot! Write a scene from your life in third person. Notice how it feels when you write about yourself this way. Does it take the emotion away? Does it lessen it at all?

Try Your Hand at Fiction

If you have started writing, or you've been too afraid to begin, you might be having second thoughts about revisiting your past. There may be some things that are just too painful to even put into words. Maybe you're nervous about sharing your story with others. But you *have* to write your story. The desire to get the words out is too strong to ignore. I hear you.

Writing your story as fiction can be helpful in this situation. The beauty with this is that only you know what is true and what is fiction. When you write your story with fictionalized elements, you are in control of not only what you share, but you have the ability to rewrite history. Is there an ex-boyfriend you've dreamed about him choking on his own vomit and having an untimely demise? Go for it! How about a bully who ruined your life? Isn't it time she got what was coming to her? She sounds like the perfect victim in your crime novel.

Using fiction to tell your story also helps distance yourself from the pain. This gives you a chance to look at it from an outsider's perception. If you are looking to sell your book, this option gives you a voice while allowing you to have privacy. The one thing to remember is if you add fictional elements to your story you can no longer call it a memoir.

Break it Down

When a piece of your story is too hard to write in complete detail, break it down into smaller pieces. When you think back to the event, writing it all out might feel overwhelming, but when you break it down, it may become manageable. Are there pieces of the story you can leave out? When you look at the event in pieces, you might see that it is not as much as you thought. Write only what you feel is important and leave everything else out. Sometimes less is more. Leave space for the reader to read between the lines. You don't have to spell everything out for every situation. You can turn something overwhelming into a sentence or two.

The exercise below will help you practice saying what you need to say with fewer words. You can get your point across without providing all the details. Think about the parts of your story you find overwhelming. Are there ways you can break them down? Are there pieces you can leave out?

Exercise:

Write your story in six words

When parts of your story become too much to write about, it is good to learn how to write in fewer words. A good way to practice this is to write your story in six words. Think about an event or a time in your life and see if you can say what you need to say in six words.

Example: *Writing my story saved my life.*

Write the events as a factual list

Another trick to write through the pain is to write the events as a factual list. Write about what happened without including any emotion or opinions. It might be helpful to write it out as a bulleted list. Just simply write the event and move on to the next one. If after you have written the list you feel more comfortable writing with more detail, you can turn the list into sentences and paragraphs that can be included in your story.

An example:

1. Stepfather hit me
2. Stepfather kicked dog
3. Stepfather threw me out of house

4. Ran to Gram's house
5. Went to friend's house
6. Told about sexual abuse
7. Talked to social worker
8. Put in foster care.

As you can see, the above list could be filled with emotion and pain. It could cause me to stop writing because it's too much to deal with in the moment. When it is written as a list of facts, it can take away the emotion attached to it and allow me to move on to the next part of my story. It also allows me to go back to the list when I feel ready and turn it into a piece of writing that fits into my story.

Change names

This sounds so simple, and maybe even unnecessary, but when I changed the names of the 'characters' in my book, I was able to write my story as an outsider. By changing the names in my story, I was able to take myself out of the story in a way. The connection I had to the person I wrote about became distant. It put the needed space between us to get the story out. When I went back to read what I had written, it helped give me more perspective into what had actually happened to me. It helped me understand what had happened actually was *that bad*. The only name I did not change was my own, but you could even do that if you decide to use a penname.

Reclaim Your Power

I hope you found some helpful tools to assist you with writing through some of your tough memories. Trauma and how it affects us is ever changing. You may think you have done the work (and you may have) and have moved past the pain only to find it is still causing you anguish. This is normal and doesn't mean you have failed. Don't try to work through the memories alone, reach out for help if you find yourself struggling. Take a break from writing for a while. Go back and read chapters two and three if you need. Most importantly, take care of yourself and listen to your needs. What do your mind, body, and spirit need? If you want to get your story out, take the time you need to honor yourself and everything you have been through.

If you don't plan on turning your story into a book, you can skip chapters eight and nine and I'll see you in chapter ten. If you decide later on to write your memoir, these chapters will give you some guidance and will be here waiting for you, if not, no pressure at all. You should be proud of the work you've done!

Power Hints:

- Burn letters you have written to people or events from your past to release the hold they have over you. Visualize the pain going up in smoke with the letter.

- If it hurts too much, stop, leave it and reflect. After you've had time to reflect, see if there is another way to write it.

Power Prompt: In what ways has your trauma made you more vulnerable, and in what ways has it made you less vulnerable?

8

Turn Your Memories into A Book

"You own everything that happened to you. Tell your stories. If people wanted you to write warmly about them, they should have behaved better." ~ **Anne Lamott**

So, you want to write a book? That's exciting, and maybe even a little terrifying, but going after something you want is incredible. When I started writing my memoir, I knew I wanted to write a book. I knew nothing else, though, not in the beginning. After I spent time getting the words out, I sat with my manuscript for a while before I took another step. I didn't know what I should do next, and I didn't know who to ask.

I had 300 pages printed out in a three-ring binder and carried it around with me, as I admired how many words I had written. I flipped through the pages and stopped long enough to read a page or two. Mortified, I closed it shut and hid it away until the desire to admire my hard work returned. I was incredibly proud of my accomplishment, but I was also terrified about the next step. Partly because I didn't even know what my next step was.

The more I read of my first draft, the more the swirl of emotion followed me. I spent a week with a highlighter and a red pen as I went through the pages in my binder. As I flipped the pages, I was at war with myself. It was crap. It was genius. Crap. Genius. Crap. Genius. I settled in the middle and pushed to the end.

One of my problems was I didn't know what it was supposed to look like. I had read a few memoirs, but none were fresh in my mind. When I wrote the 300 pages in my hand, I had not thought about anyone reading it, which makes no sense since my goal was always to publish it. I didn't write my first draft with readers in mind. The only thing on my mind was getting the words out. That was it.

I hadn't considered what my theme was, or what message I wanted the readers to take away, and I sure didn't consider making it flow like a narrative. Essentially, I had written over one hundred thousand words in my diary. As I read it I noticed how much it was lacking, but I also saw the potential on the pages.

After reading through the entire manuscript, I found an editor after many hours of researching and digging through pages of search results on the internet. After talking with the editor and paying the down payment to hold my spot, I read through the pages one last time. I remember tossing the binder to the ground as I sat by the community pool my kids were splashing around in and thinking it was hopeless. There was no way I was going to be able to turn my words into anything. I shoved the binder into the tote bag and joined my kids in the pool.

When I got home, I put the binder on my desk and walked away from it. A few days later, my editor said she had an opening and could begin on my manuscript earlier than she thought. I stared at the screen and read her words over and over again. That fear and negative self-talk had returned, but there was something louder. Something that told me to "send it." I closed my eyes and pushed the air out of my lungs. I attached the word document and hit 'send.' A wave of dread washed over me. What if she hates it? What if I just wasted my money?

I shook all the negative thoughts out of my head and went about my life. Full disclosure, I actually refreshed my email a hundred times a day to see if my editor had returned my manuscript early, but I didn't let the self-doubting thoughts take over. The dread switched to excitement. I was ready to hear what I needed to do to turn my words into a book.

When I received my manuscript back, my editor warned me about all the 'red' marks I would see. She explained to me I had a lot of great information and she enjoyed my voice. I tried to take her warning and not get my feelings hurt, but the voice reminding me how horrible I am at everything crept back in. I shook it out of my head and focused on her remarks. I saw my problem; I had written my entire story as if it were a journal entry. There was no real flow to the story. It was just an account of everything I had been through. My editor assured me I had the writing ability to turn this document into a book people would want to read. She encouraged me to rewrite it and follow her suggestions.

One suggestion was to cut out over thirty thousand words. That was the most painful blow of all. There was no way I could throw away that many words. The thought alone was devastating. How would I remove that many words? When I wrote my story, I felt like every word was important. I was partially right. Every word was an important part of my healing and releasing my pain. It was what I needed to do to reclaim my power, but not every word was important to the message I wanted readers to take away. I was looking at the two processes as one, when they were two separate parts. One was for me, the other was for the reader. When I was able to understand this, I was able to take some of my editor's suggestions at face value and didn't let them destroy me.

The thought of having to rewrite the entire book was devastating, but it was also motivating because I was one step closer to having a physical copy of my book in my hand. For me, writing the memoir version of my story was equally exhausting as writing the first draft. This was because when I went back through to turn my experiences into narrative nonfiction, I had to reenact the events I was writing about. I closed my eyes and almost dropped myself back in time. I became the five-year-old who watched my father physically attack my older brother, and I wrote about it from her perspective. I wanted every word I wrote to count. I wanted to make sure the readers felt the horror, pain, heartache, and desperation with me, so they would then experience the healing along with me.

Writing your memoir will be a much different experience than writing the events that have caused you pain. It will encompass much of the same information, but it will be written differently. There are a few things to consider when turning your story into a memoir. We'll go over some of the most important pieces in the next sections.

What will your theme be?

When writing a memoir, it's important for it to have a theme. The theme is the message you want the readers to take away. Some people describe the theme as the heartbeat or soul of the book. When asked what a book is about some people get plot and theme confused. The plot is what happens, where the theme is why it happens, and why you are telling your story.

Your story is about lessons, learning, and growth. The theme of your story is to help solve problems for the readers. Readers pick books they feel will offer them something. It could be learning they are not alone or even just for entertainment. A reader needs a reason to pick up a book, your theme will help them determine if it is a book they will spend their time with.

Some examples of themes are:

- Love never dies
- Never give up

- Keep going after your dreams
- You can heal your life
- Small things are beautiful
- Loss
- Recovery from accident/illness
- Loneliness
- Survival
- Romance after disappointment
- Faith against the odds
- Coming back to oneself
- Addressing trauma/adverse childhood experiences
- Accepting change

What will your theme be? What do you want the reader to take away from reading your story?

Setting

I wrote my entire memoir without mentioning where the story took place. I knew where it happened; I knew where I lived. It didn't seem like something I needed to mention. When I received my manuscript back from my editor, she asked me what the setting was. She explained without letting the readers know where the story took place, things that were important to the story would be less impactful. Just because I knew where my story took place doesn't mean the reader will.

An example brought to my attention was when I wrote about getting my driver's license and how it gave me freedom. She said without explaining the story took place in a rural setting; it took the power from that moment away. If the story took place in the city, having a driver's license wouldn't have been as pivotal for finding my freedom because there are other forms of transportation but living in a rural area, it was my only form of transportation. Something as simple as that can change the entire story. A life-changing moment in your story may become insignificant if readers don't know where the story takes place.

Showing your setting doesn't have to take a lot of time. You can add a simple sentence about living in a small town or life in the city. All it takes is a few words to pull the reader into your world. Use descriptive words and show the readers where you live. Open up your world to them, invite them in and help them get acquainted.

Your Voice

Before I started writing, I didn't understand what showing your voice in writing meant. I thought all I had to do was write. And, in a sense, that's true. But you also have to be you by including your personality, character, passion and emotion. Your voice will set your tone and will convey your message in your own unique way. This will help the reader get to know you. The best advice to help you find your voice is to just be you, don't try too hard to be anything else. Your writing voice will emerge as you find yourself and your actual voice.

Structure

Memoirs differ from journaling because a memoir has a beginning, a middle, and an ending. Journaling is free writing that does not need to follow any set rules or guidelines. Memoirs are shared with others, while journals are often for your eyes only. Memoirs must contain conflict, rising action, a crisis, a climax and a resolution. Something significant happens in each scene. Memoirs are written much like novels; except they are true.

Outline

You've probably had to create an outline at least once while in school. People tend to either love them or hate them, but they can be a very useful tool when writing your memoir. An outline will help you remember everything you want to include in your story and help you get a plan in place.

An outline can be as simple as a few words to as complex as several pages. It will give you a plan to follow. It is compared to a blueprint or map for your story. When you use an outline, you can skip around in your story. When you have an idea where you want the story to go, it will be easier to stay on task. It will also ensure you include everything that is important to telling your story.

An outline is not set in stone. It is changeable and moveable. As you start writing, your vision and plan may change. When I wrote my first outline for my memoir, it was very simple. I wrote the key topics I wanted to include and placed them in the place I thought they would fit the best. As I was writing my story, I used the outline as a guide. When I went back through my manuscript and did my rewrite, I also made a new outline.

Sample Simple Outline:

Introduction: What the story is about/theme
Chapter One
Chapter Two
Chapter Three
Chapter Four
Chapter Five
Chapter Six
Chapter Seven
Chapter Eight
Chapter Nine
Chapter Ten/Conclusion: How your life is now/how the problem was solved/dealt with

You can use the above simple format to complete your outline quickly. It may be all you need to get started and stay on track. A quick search online will help you find a more detailed example. Find an example that works for you and your story.

When you complete your outline, just place the topics you want to include in each chapter. You can move it around and add topics where you want them. This outline is for you, no one else needs to see it. Give yourself the freedom to get creative and make mistakes and take chances. Everything is fixable.

Hero's Journey

The Hero's Journey is a popular structure for writing memoirs. It is based on Joseph Campbell's Monomyth. The monomyth is the structure of the universal human journey. Movies such as *Star Wars*, *The Matrix*, and *The Lion King* have used this structure. You can find out more about this in Campbell's book, *The Hero with a Thousand Faces*.

A quick overview of the structure is below:

1. The Ordinary World: The hero (or heroine) exists in their normal world. He often doesn't feel he fits in. He possesses characteristics that make him feel out of place, or out of the ordinary.
2. The Call of Adventure: The hero receives an invitation, message, or challenge calling him to something greater.
3. Refusal of the Call: The hero may be reluctant to leave the ordinary world behind or he may question his capability or even desire to fulfill the task at hand. In the end, he accepts his destiny.
4. Meeting the Mentor: Once he has committed to the quest, the mentor appears, or becomes known. The mentor provides the tools needed to move forward in the face of the unknown.
5. Crossing the First Threshold: The hero acts

upon his call to adventure and crosses the threshold from his ordinary world, into the new world.

6. Tests, Allies, Enemies: Out of his comfort zone, the hero is confronted with a difficult series of challenges. He runs into obstacles while his skills are tested to their limits. He gains deeper insight into his own character. He also finds out who can be trusted and who can't. He may earn allies and meet enemies who will, each in their own way, help prepare him for the challenges to come.

7. Approach to the Inmost Cave: The hero faces danger, or an inner conflict that, up until now, he has not had to face. As he approaches the danger, he must prepare before taking that final leap into the great unknown.

8. The Ordeal: The hero faces a dangerous physical test or a deep inner crisis that he must face to survive. He must face his greatest fear and draw upon all of his skills and experiences to overcome his most difficult challenge. This is where everything the hero holds dear is put on the line. If he fails, he will either die, or life as he knows it will never be the same again.

9. Reward (Seizing the Sword): After defeating the enemy, surviving death, and overcoming his greatest personal challenge, the hero is ultimately transformed into a new, stronger person.

10. The Road Back: The hero's journey is not yet over. He may need one last push back into the Ordinary World. The moment before he finally commits to the last stage of his journey may be a moment in which he must choose between his own personal objective, and that of a Higher Cause.

11. Resurrection: This is the climax, in which the hero has his most dangerous and final encounter with death. The final battle represents something greater than his own existence. The outcome has widespread consequences that reach into the ordinary world, as well as the lives of those left behind. If he fails, others will suffer. Ultimately, he will succeed by destroying his enemy. He will emerge from battle cleansed and reborn.

12. Return with the Elixir: The hero returns to the Ordinary World as a changed person. He has grown and learned many things from facing many dangers, including even death, however he now looks forward to the start of a new life. He is now a hero.

When looking at your story, can you see how your journey follows these steps? Does it help you look at your story differently?

What will your title be?

Have you given any thought to the title of your memoir? This can be hard to come up with, or it is something you knew even before you started writing. Most writers will figure out the title during the writing process. It will either just come to you, or a line or passage in your book will pop out to you and you'll know.

Before I started writing my memoir, I knew the title I

wanted. I was so set on this title that I even made pens and a mug with the name and photo I wanted to use on the cover. I happily sent my manuscript to my editor, and she wrote back with a note next to the title, "You may want to reconsider this. No one will know what your book is about." Of course, it gutted me. I *knew* this was my title. It had to be. After I let the dust settle and picked up the pieces of my heart, I knew she was right. My original title was *Moonlit Madness: A Journey Through Darkness Guided by the Light Within*. My argument was I traveled through unimaginable darkness, and I loved the moon... so why not? The reader wouldn't know what I was trying to say.

The next few days I agonized over the perfect title. I laid awake for nights trying to figure it out. My eyes were wide open as I stared into the darkness. Nothing came. My husband talked it over with me and suggested, "How about *The Monster That Ate My Mommy*?" To be honest, I didn't love it, but I could make sense of it. This was something my mom used to say to me when I was a child and it also explained how depression took her from me. It grew on me and eventually became my title.

There are still times I wonder about the title. At book signings people will often pick the book up and giggle at the title. "This looks fun," they snicker as I look at them with a smile and assure them it's not. "If you enjoy reading about child abuse and death, then it's a blast." This ends with them putting the book back on the table as they muster up a fake smile before they disappear. This explains why titles are so important.

My title doesn't have a subtitle. It lets the reader

know it's a memoir, but that's all. If they want to find out what the book is about, they have to read the back cover, which is what you want to have happen. The longer they spend with your book, the more likely they will feel a connection to it or decide it's not the book for them. Both options are good. You don't want your book to fall into the wrong hands. I would not want young children to read my book, or someone who has unresolved trauma. However, I want someone who needs to hear my story to find my book. Your title can help with this.

A title is your first line of marketing. You want something that relates to your book. You might consider including a subtitle to give a little more explanation to what your book is about. Think of something that you will be comfortable talking about, and not be embarrassed every time you have to tell someone. It should have a connection to the book.

If you need help coming up with a title, you can save it until the end. You can also ask others for help coming up with suggestions. It's helpful to keep a list of all possible ideas. It might surprise you when the perfect title will appear. It is a lot like finding the perfect name for your child. After all, writing is a labor of love!

Writing Tips

Dialogue

Some writers despise using dialogue when they write. It's one of my favorite parts of the story to write! When my characters talk to each other, they start to come alive!

When my editor told me I needed to include dialogue in my memoir, my heart sank. I worried I wouldn't be able to make the people in my life sound like themselves, but the more I used it, the more fun I had with my story.

When you use dialogue in your writing, make sure the conversations sound natural. After you write a section, go back and read it aloud. Does it flow like a regular conversation or does it sound forced? Some advice I was given that helped me make it flow better was to go to a coffee shop and eavesdrop. Listen in to the conversations around you and get a feel for what is being said and how it is said. When people talk, they most likely use contractions. People don't say, "I did not like the movie. It was not my favorite. Do not make me watch it again!" They might say, "I didn't like the movie. It wasn't my favorite. Don't make me watch it again!"

It is also important to make the 'characters' in your book have their own voice. You will have your author voice, but the people you are writing about should have their own voice, too. When you write out a conversation you had with a character in your book, close your eyes and try to hear them saying the words. After you write it, read it out loud and see if it sounds like them. There is an art to dialogue, but it shouldn't be feared. With practice it can really bring your characters to life, and help readers get to know who they are reading about.

Show Don't Tell

Show, don't tell is one of the most important pieces of information to learn about writing. It is what brings your words off the page and into the reader's heart. When you show, you are letting the reader experience everything you went through. It is what can turn a good book into a great book. When you effectively show, readers will experience the emotions along with you. Show the readers the story using all five senses.

Tip: Use fewer **"*tell*"** words. I heard. I felt. I saw.

Example:

Telling: *Rebecca was afraid of the dark.*
Showing: *When Rebecca's mom turned off the light and left the room, Rebecca tensed. She hid under the covers and held her breath as the floorboard in the hall creaked.*

Notice the use of repeated words

Most writers have a few words they overuse. One of my favorites is *that*. I try to be aware of the use of this word while I am writing, but I don't focus too much on it. When I am finished with my first draft and it is time to edit, I search for the word in question in the document. I go through and cut out as many as I can.

It is also a good idea to go through your document and look for the same word repeated in the section. Let's say you are writing about houses. You can use the words houses, homes, residences, dwellings, domiciles, quarters, or buildings. If you get stuck, pull out a thesaurus and pick some different words to use. This is a great step to save for the editing stage, but if you notice it as you're writing see what you can come up with.

Before and after

Your memoir should illustrate the difference between who you are now versus who you were then. It should highlight what you learned along the way and it should show the internal and external obstacles that shaped you along the way. Readers want to see that you overcame the struggle, so they know they can, too. This is also important for you to pay attention to so you can see how far you have come. Be proud of your before and after.

Memoir tips

Be kind to yourself

This is the most important tip. You are probably going to remember things from your life that you would have liked to forget. Things you are not proud of or you're ashamed of will flash before your eyes. Life is filled with ups and downs, don't let the memories control you. You are not the event that happened. You have grown and learned along the way. As you write your memoir, remember to have compassion for yourself. If it had happened to someone else, would you be so hard on them? Give yourself as much love as you would anyone else.

Just write

Don't judge what you've written and don't second guess yourself. Get everything out, no matter how awful, embarrassing or painful it is.

Turn off your inner critic

"I'm not a good enough writer to write this." "It wasn't that bad." "Maybe it didn't happen that way." When these thoughts come, try your best to push them out. At this stage it's important to just get the words out. Don't strive for perfection. Everything can be changed later.

Take it one day at a time

Take the process one day at a time, one story at a time, one word at a time. Try to write every day, even just a few minutes, but don't push yourself. You'll reach your goal as long as you keep going.

Get support

Ask for help when you need it. Find an accountability partner who will help you stay focused. Tell your friends about your writing goal. If you need a writing coach to help you keep going, do some research and find someone you'll be comfortable working with. If you're having a hard time with the subject matter, work with a counselor or healer to help you through the trauma and memories that come.

Don't give up

When you're stuck, don't give up. Remember your why for wanting to write your story. Think about how great you'll feel when you are able to hold the finished product in your hands.

Write each chapter as a short story

If you look at every chapter as a short story you'll be able to break the big project up into smaller, more manageable pieces. Every chapter should have a beginning, middle, and end.

Make each chapter a new document

If you make a new document for each chapter, it will make it more manageable. It will also be easier to move chapters around. Make sure you save your work in multiple locations. When I worked on my memoir, I saved my documents to a thumb drive, emailed a copy to myself and also saved it on my computer. If you add the date to the saved title, you will know which one is your latest version.

What you write is yours

What you write is yours to do what you want with. If

you decide you don't want to share your finished story with anyone, you don't have to. If you want to share your story but don't want to include certain events or memories, you don't have to. You are in control of your story now. You have the say in what you share and what you don't.

Memoir mistakes

Thinking writing a memoir is easy

Some people may think writing a memoir is easy. I thought it would be easier than writing fiction. I was wrong! I found it so much easier to make up a story and create the world they lived in than to make sense of what I had lived through. I can understand why it seems easier, but when I write fiction, I feel freer to take the story wherever it leads me. I let the characters take over and tell their stories. I do write about characters who have faced real-life issues, many of which I have also experienced, so in a sense the stories do resemble pieces of my life.

Fiction is easier for me because, although it is filled with emotions, they do not have to be my emotions. The characters are not real people and they haven't actually been hurt. When I wrote my memoir, I worried about what I shared. I wondered if I shared too much or not enough. I worried readers would be too upset by what I wrote or what I didn't write. When readers left comments or reviews about my life, it was more personal than it is when they offer feedback on the fiction stories.

Writing your memoir is hard. You may not have to make up the setting or the characters, but you may have to experience feelings and trauma you might not have thought about for years.

Turning your memoir into an autobiography

Another common memoir mistake people make is turning their memoir into an autobiography. An autobiography is your life story in its entirety. It starts at birth and covers the events up to the present. It will be written with more facts and less narrative. Most readers are only interested in reading autobiographies of famous people, where they enjoy memoirs from everyday people.

Including the small and trivial

Another common mistake when writing a memoir is including small, unimportant details that don't move the story along. Readers don't want to know about every item you bought when you went on vacation when you were twelve.

Bragging

Readers are turned off by bragging. While they want to cheer you on in the story, they need to be able to relate to you. No one likes someone who brags. You should be proud of your accomplishments but share them in a way that doesn't come off vain. Think about that friend who you dread hearing them tell you a story because you know it's going to lead to them telling you how amazing they are. No one likes that, and no one wants to read about it.

Preaching

If you have a message to share with your readers do it in a way they don't feel you are preaching to them. Let the reader make up their own mind as they read your story. Don't try to change their mind or their beliefs.

Using the wrong tone

When you write your memoir it's important to use your voice, but there is a time and place for a sarcastic or funny tone. You can add sarcasm or humor, but make sure it fits with the story. Make sure you use the correct tone to get the point across you want to make. Be sure you aren't condescending; readers will pick up on it and most likely put your book down.

First drafts

First drafts are not meant to be perfect. They are meant to be full of messy emotions and mistakes. This is your first attempt to release your words and your pain. Your primary objective with your first draft should just be to finish it.

When you stop to read your work, you can lose your focus. Your internal critic can take over and tell you how awful it is. The negative self-talk can creep back in and whisper how much it sucks and tell you not to finish. You can get stuck. Turn your self critic off and keep writing until you reach the end.

Get to the end and take a deep breath. Give yourself a pat on the back. You did it! Now that you've celebrated this accomplishment, set the document aside. Give yourself some distance from the words you just wrote. Use your time to do some self-care activities you weren't able to when you were so focused on writing.

Take as much time away from your writing as you need. After I finished my first draft, I tucked it away for almost a year. I needed a break from the raw emotions on the pages. I needed to forget my story and clear my head. The time you take is up to you, but don't rush into it. It will be there when you're ready.

When some time has passed, you can then go back through your first draft and give it a read through. Don't be too hard on yourself. Anything that you're unhappy with can be fixed. Just take it one word at a time.

A quote I love about first drafts by Shannon Hale is, *"I'm writing a first draft and reminding myself that I'm simply shoveling sand into a box so that I can later build sandcastles."* If you don't write the words, you won't have anything to shape into the sandcastle that will become your book. So, go get your sand pail and start shoveling that sand into it. You've got this!

Self-editing

After you have given your first draft some time to sit,

it's time to go back through it. You will want to read the entire manuscript, starting from the beginning. Everyone has their own way of editing, so find what works best for you. My method for self-editing is I print out the complete manuscript and put it in a 3-ring binder. I have a highlighter and red pen and begin to read. I read through once to see how the story flows and quickly mark errors that catch my attention. I then go back through and look for and make a note of any:

- spelling errors
- punctuation errors
- misused words
- overused words
- incorrect information/fact check
- information that is out of order

When I have gone through my manuscript twice, I take the corrections I have made a note of and make the changes in the document. Another step you can take is to have it read out loud to you by the computer or read it out loud to yourself. You will be able to hear any mistakes you have missed.

Self-editing is an important step to take before you send it off to an editor. This step may take you a lot of time, but it will save you money and give you the opportunity to remove any information you don't want to include in the final story. There will still be mistakes and corrections because you are too close to the story to catch them all. However, when you fix all the mistakes you can find before sending it to an editor, you are sending your best work.

In the final stage of your writing your book, you will decide what you include and what you leave out. The best advice I can offer you if you want to heal is to write everything. Write like no one will see it and then go back through and pick what you leave in to share. This way you are able to accomplish two things; writing to heal and writing your book. Just because something made its way into your first draft does not mean it has to be seen by anyone else.

If after you have written your book and you decide you don't want to share it outside of your family and friends, there are printing companies that can help you accomplish this. Lulu, at http://www.lulu.com is a company I have used with great results. Just be careful you do not check the box that allows it to be distributed. There may be local options in your area, as well. The finished products from these sites are just as beautiful as the books being sold in bookstores. This will allow you to control who you share your story with.

If you are interested in publishing your book for it to be shared with a much wider audience, you will want to read the next chapter.

Power Hints:

- Read other memoirs before you write your final draft. It will give you a feel for what readers are looking for.
- Look at every chapter as a short story.
- Start a new document for every chapter.

Power Prompt: The family secrets I am supposed to keep are…

9

When You're Ready to Publish Your Story

"You must never be fearful about what you are doing when it is right." ~*Rosa Parks*

Publishing your memoir is a mountain to climb all on its own, but it is not one that's impossible to climb. Now that you have your completed manuscript, and it has been edited, it is time to consider your options. It is easier than ever to turn your manuscript into a book. Just hop onto Amazon.com and take a look at all the books listed for sale. People's dreams are coming true every day with just a few clicks of a mouse.

Before I started the voyage from writer to author, I was intimidated by all that I needed to figure out. When I didn't know the needed steps, it felt unachievable. I didn't even know where to start. My dream was stronger than the fear. Every day I spent hours researching what I needed to do to become a published author. I soon learned I had three options to choose from. Search for an agent to represent me, work with a hybrid press, or do it all on my own.

When I looked into what I needed to do to work with an agent and work with a traditional publisher, I knew it was not the route I wanted to take. This was mostly because I had a goal to have my memoir published in 2017, and it would have taken longer than I wanted to wait. Working with an agent required additional steps of querying an agent. Querying an agent is a needed step when you hope to have your memoir picked up by a publisher.

Looking for a literary agent can sometimes take years to find a good fit. It depends on many things, many of which are out of the author's control. If the agent is not looking for your style of memoir, they will not be able to work with you. If they dislike your style of writing, they may pass on you. It is very possible you will receive rejections from many agents. It is also possible that you will not hear back from some agents you have queried. This is all normal and part of the process. It was not one I wanted to spend time on when I was eager to publish my memoir.

The most enticing choice was working with a hybrid publisher. These publishers have also been known as vanity presses. There are many types of hybrid presses and you will need to do your research before you decide to work with one. A quick search online will yield some very disheartening results of horror stories when authors did not take the needed time to ask questions and read reviews from other customers. When you work with a hybrid press, you typically do not need to be accepted by an agent, or anyone else. You simply need to pick the package you're interested in and pay the fee. There is obviously much more to it than that, and each one is different, but that's the main idea.

The one I had looked into was going to cost me well over two thousand dollars, and I would have needed to provide the company with an edited manuscript. For the money they would have provided my memoir with a cover, formatted the document, and uploaded it to the proper places to have my book available for sale online. I spoke with an associate of the company I was excited to work with. They told me I would be able to hold my book in my hand in a matter of weeks. All I had to do was sign a contract, make the down payment, and submit my manuscript.

When I learned how much money I needed to complete this task, my excitement fizzled out. In order to help with my disappointment, I started digging deeper online to find out information about the company. I wanted to know if it was really worth all that money for what they would do for me. As the search results populated, I was relieved to know I had not jumped into something I wouldn't be able to get out of. My desire to have a finished product took away my logic in the moment. Everything the company was offering me was something I could figure out how to do myself for a fraction of the cost.

When these two options became out of my reach, I knew I would have to do it on my own. I spent many hours online researching everything I needed to know to self-publish my book. Since my manuscript had been edited, I didn't need to do this step. I needed a cover designer and someone to format the inside of my book. Both of these items can vary in price, and there are programs that will help you do these tasks yourself. For me, getting some of the responsibility out of my hands and paying someone who already had these skills was more than worth it for me.

After I had the inside and outside of my book completed, there was more to learn. Every time I thought I had it figured out, there was something else to learn. At every turn there was a new challenge, but everything I needed to know was available with a search online. If I had questions, I reached out to some people I met in the writing communities and found the answers to all of my questions.

After a few months of finding information and applying it to my book and setting up accounts, I was ready to self-publish my memoir. I am hopeful I can share enough to make the process easier for you. When you've come this far, you're too close to give up.

Legal Issues

Chances are if you are writing a book about trauma you experienced, other people were involved. The question that comes is will you get sued? The most honest answer I can give is, I have no idea. I am not a lawyer and I do not know the law around this, but I can share with you what I learned as I went through this process.

After I wrote the first draft of my memoir, the feeling I felt after pure excitement was dread. When I read through the pages I had just written, I didn't know what I was going to do. There were so many people I included in my story I was sure at least someone was going to sue me. I feverishly searched the internet for answers to the question: Can I get sued for writing about someone in my memoir? The answers I found were inconsistent. It seemed every site I went to had a different answer.

I learned if I wrote about someone who had died, there would be no chance of litigation. This answer seemed to remain consistent. Most people I wrote about in my memoir were dead. I felt a little sigh of relief, but I still didn't trust it. The next thing I read was if you have proof of what you are stating in your book there is no way you will get sued. Again, I was not confident with this answer.

When I reached out to a lawyer (not just the FAQ section of the webpage), I was told in order to be free from litigation I needed to change all names and identifying characteristics, or the people and places included in my book. I was also told I could not make things up. Everything had to be true, and I had to be able to prove them. He ended the conversation by telling me there was always a chance someone may sue me. Great.

Defeated, I stared at my manuscript and considered my options. The first thing I did was change all the names in my book. Living or dead, everyone except me received a new name. Surprisingly, this helped more than I could have imagined. When I read my story with these new names, my story became almost fictionalized. For the first time in my life, I was able to step outside of my story and see it as an outsider. This is when my holy cow moment came. This was when I finally realized how bad it had been. I was able to understand how close I had been to death at the hands of another. This act alone gave me more power over my story. It took the emotion out of it and made me want to get my story out into the world even more.

Changing names may not be the solution you need to feel comfortable sharing your story. You may consider using a penname. A penname is when you use a different name when you publish your book. This helps separate your personal life from your author life. There are plenty of authors who use pennames. You will need to decide if you want to put a face to your name, or if you want to keep your privacy. This may be tricky if you plan on speaking about your book or having an online presence.

If there is a person you are worried about coming after you for telling your story, consider asking their permission. It would be best to do this in writing, and even better if it is done with a lawyer. This is not always a feasible option. Often the people who end up in our stories are people who have caused some sort of harm to us. If asking permission puts your safety at risk, this is not the route you should take.

The other option is to fictionalize your story. It would no longer be classified as a memoir, but you would be the only person who would know what pieces were true and what parts were embellished. If you have your heart set on writing your memoir, this is not the best option.

The last piece of advice that came from the lawyer was, when in doubt, leave it out. If you are still unsure what to do, seek legal advice. There are ways around most areas of concern. Don't let fear control you, but also be prepared for all possibilities.

Will You Self publish?

When I first started writing my memoir, I didn't know how it was going to become a book. I spent months researching different ways to turn my words into a book I could hold in my hands. My search led me to an option I felt I could manage, but the cost was way out of my comfort level. When I read the fine print, I learned the cost would not get me much of anything. I still needed to find an editor, and some sites I even needed to provide my own cover. Cover? How do I even go about making a book cover?

The searches expanded and with everything I found; I uncovered something else I needed to consider. I found some Facebook groups for authors and sifted through the content. I found people in these groups who had been where I was. I asked about the companies I had been considering, even though I didn't know how I was going to pay for the fee. Multiple people commented and warned me to stay away. I was told it should never cost money, outside of an editor, formatter and cover designer.

I asked more questions. Where do I find an editor? Where do I find a cover designer? What in the world is a formatter? Each question I asked was met with kindness, and I figured out what I needed to do to turn the words on my computer screen into a book with actual pages.

I joined more writing groups and found an editor to

work with. I read her reviews and did a search online to see if there had been any complaints or scams. When everything checked out, I paid her half of the agreed upon fee and my manuscript. After talking with her, she was able to connect me with a cover designer to help design the book cover. More conversations led to finding a formatter, which was the person who turns the manuscript into a file that can be uploaded in a program to create the actual book.

When I had these pieces in place, it was time to decide where I wanted my book to be sold. At the time Create Space was the print on demand company for Amazon (it has since been changed to Kindle Direct Publishing or KDP). If I just wanted to print my book within Amazon, I did not need to buy an ISBN (a what? I'll tell you soon!). If I did not want my book to be available anywhere else, I was ready to get the process started.

If I wanted to have my book available for purchase at bookstores and libraries, I needed to use Ingram Spark. This choice led me to needing to purchase the ISBN after all, as well as a few more steps, which I will list below.

The entire process was overwhelming and could very easily become my full-time job. Without help from other authors and my editor I am not sure I would have been able to figure the process out. It wasn't overly difficult, but there were so many steps I had no idea I needed to take.

If this seems overwhelming just reading about it, or you don't know where to start, the companies I first talked about, which are known as vanity presses, might be the best option for you. They do a lot of the work for you and depending on their fee, they may do all of it. It would be best to do your research and ask other authors who have used them for their input. A quick search online should give you enough information to help you decide.

A Quick Guide to Self-Publishing

This is a quick guide to self-publishing. It will not answer every question you have, but it should give you enough information to make an informed decision.

1. Write your manuscript
2. Edit your manuscript (at the very least read through it to make sure you have corrected as many errors as you see)
3. Find an editor (there are different types of editors: line editors, copy editors, and proofreaders)
4. Find a cover designer. It is best to work with someone who is familiar with the type of book you have written (in this case, memoir). When you work with a cover artist, they will ask you if you want an e-book and a print book. There will generally be a fee for both. If you are going to have a paperback, you will need to determine what size you want it to be. Some standard sizes include 6x9 and 5x8.
5. Find someone who can format your manuscript (they will need to format it for a

print copy and an e-book). They will also need to know what size your book is.

6. Decide if you want to publish on Kindle Direct Publishing, most commonly known as KDP can be found at: https://kdp.amazon.com and Ingram Spark publishing can be found at: https://myaccount.ingramspark.com/Account/Signup. There are other print on demand services available, but KDP and Ingram Spark are the two I have used and seem to be most used by other self-published authors. They both have a slight learning curve to them but are mostly easy to use. If you run into any problems, there is help available either on the site or in writing communities online.

7. If you just go with KDP, you are ready to publish!

8. If you want to add your book to other locations, you will need to purchase an International Standard Book Number (ISBN). An ISBN is essentially a product identifier. Publishers, booksellers, libraries, internet retailers and other supply chain participants use it for ordering, listing, sales records and stock control purposes. The ISBN identifies the registrant (you in the case of self-publishing) as well as the specific title, edition and format. If you plan on publishing your book in more than one format (paperback, hardcover, audiobook and eBook) you will

need an ISBN for each format. When you purchase an ISBN, you will need to make an account. When you create your account, you will be able to create your own publishing company that can be listed in your book and online. In the United States, you can purchase an ISBN or a pack of them go to: https://www.myidentifiers.com/identify-protect-your-book/isbn/buy-isbn.

9. You may also want to consider getting a Library of Congress number to include on the inside cover of your book. This is free and will place your book in the Library of Congress online catalogue. When you request a number, it is for print books only and must be entered on the copyright page in your book. To apply go to: https://www.loc.gov/.

10. If you want to apply for copyright, you can do this now, as well (there is a fee involved). Some people suggest you do not need a copyright because once your book is written you own the rights to the document while others feel it is important to copyright their work. To file for copyright go to: https://www.copyright.gov/.

11. Market, market, market (although, if your goal is to be seen and make money, this step should be at the top of the list). Social media is a big part of having an online presence as is having a website. If you get a website, it is best to use your name and not the title of

your book. You will always be you, but you may write more books.

Will You Look for an Agent?

If self-publishing doesn't sound like something you want to invest your time in, you can consider working with a traditional publisher. To go this route, you will most likely need to find an agent to represent you. When you work with an agent, you will not have as much control over your book as you would if you self-publish. You will also need to pay your agent a percentage of the royalties from book sales.

Some writers query agents hoping to land a deal, and some do, but others are not so lucky. I did not even attempt to work with an agent for my memoir. I had given myself a date to have my book released, and I didn't want to wait for someone else. When you work with a traditional publisher, chances are your book will not be published for at least a year, and often longer. If after receiving rejections or being unable to find the perfect fit, you can still self-publish. There is nothing wrong with trying to work with an agent, just as there is nothing wrong with self-publishing. To each their own.

OMG! Everyone will know my story!

When my book went live and was available to be read by other people I went into a depression. I thought I was ready to share my story with the world and I had been excited to finally be free of the secrets I had been holding onto. I was not prepared for the emotions that swept over me when my book was available for purchase. Those negative voices that had been so loud before returned. I heard them tell me things like what a piece of garbage my book was and how no one wanted to read my story.

The negative thoughts were not the only upsetting thing that happened to me during the process. I also felt naked. Completely naked. Every secret I had spilled on the pages of my memoir had been set free. Anyone who wanted to take the time to read my story would know. They would know all the things I had worked so hard for most of my life to keep hidden. They would know all of my failures and missed opportunities. The vulnerability I felt made me feel like the helpless child I had been so many years before. I couldn't breathe. Panic filled my body. *What did I do?* It was too late. My story was out there. My lifelong dream had come true.

I went into a sort of hiding, if only within myself. I felt embarrassed, and the last thing I wanted to do was tell anyone about this book. I didn't celebrate the publishing of my memoir, at least not right away. I didn't tell people I worked with and I didn't mention it unless I needed to. A friend of mine and my mentor published her memoir just days before I published mine. She played a huge roll in my healing journey and I watched her celebrate. I even went to her book signing for her release party.

When I walked up to congratulate her and ask her to sign my copy of her book, she asked me about mine. The embarrassment returned, and I hung my head. I knew she wanted to celebrate my accomplishment, too. Within a week we had planned a launch party for my book, and she agreed to join me. With her help, I was able to celebrate the one accomplishment I had been so desperate to cross on my bucket list.

At the party there were people I didn't know, and they had read my book. The voice I had worked so hard to find felt like it was going to take off. A sense of panic settled over me as I looked out into the audience and saw all eyes on me. And then I read. I read parts of my story and felt alive. When the questions came, I found out how much my story had touched them, and how much it had helped some people there. People related to the trauma I had survived, and it gave them hope that they, too, could share their story one day. And here we are.

I want to tell you that it's scary when your story first gets released. The part of us that wants us to fail tries to take over, but I'll tell you right now that is not what matters. What matters is that you did it. You were able to get the words out of your head and let the power they held over you diminish, if only a little. You still won. You still came out on top. I know when people read your story they are going to be moved. They are going to feel the emotions you worked so hard to extract from your heart and placed on the page.

That crown and cape I mentioned at the beginning of the book, that's yours now. Wear it with pride and honor. Know you are in great company. Your story will not only help you, but it will also inspire others. Let the feelings of vulnerability come, embrace the fear, but shake it off. You control the power now.

Do you want to buy my book?

That's the question you might start asking after your book is available for sale. If you're like me, you might feel yourself die a little inside when you pose the question. You've been working hard on healing and finding your voice, now you need to step completely out of your comfort zone and market your book, which in turn means selling yourself (your story).

I published my memoir in early September and after doing my research, I reached out to bookstores in my area. I live in a small town, so my options were limited. The closest Barnes and Noble is two hours away, but everything I read led me to believe I needed to go. I emailed the bookstore manager a few times, and they set a signing up for me a few weeks before Christmas. I had a few weeks to get myself mentally prepared for the event and had some bookmarks and some other freebies to hand out. My anxiety was through the roof. I told myself it would be fine, there was nothing to worry about.

The days slipped away and before I knew it, it was finally the day. My husband and I got up early to arrive at the bookstore on time. Two hours away meant I didn't know anyone in the area. I tried to talk myself into believing this was a good thing. Since I lived most of my life (okay, all of it) as an introvert, the thought of talking with strangers became too much.

When we arrived at the bookstore, the manager I had

been talking with was off for the day and another staff member came to help me set up. I was given a small table in the middle of the store and was told I needed to engage the customers. Engage the customers? What did that even mean? My anxiety was replaced with panic. The room started to spin, and I had to hold on to the table to keep my balance. I felt my old self arrive and push out all the work I had done. The timid little girl felt the world crash down around her.

I took a deep breath and reminded myself it was only four hours. Four hours in a busy bookstore a few days before Christmas. I pushed up the biggest smile I could make and held out bookmarks to the people walking by. "Hi, would you like a bookmark?" Surprisingly, the most common answer was, "no." With every rejection, I felt myself start to shrink. I did not want to be there any longer. A battle between who I used to be and who I was becoming took place inside of me. I jumped out of my comfort zone that day and learned just how hard it is to sell myself.

When I got people to engage in conversation, I assured them they didn't want to read my book right now. It was too sad to read right before Christmas. That was not the best sales pitch! This tactic did work with one woman, and I sold one book that day. One painful sale. But I learned a lot about the process and myself. This was just another step in figuring out who I was and what I wanted.

I walked away from that bookstore feeling empowered. After four hours of feeling like time had stood still, I knew I could do anything. Maybe it wasn't what I expected it to look like, but I put myself out there and gave it my best shot. It might have been awkward, but I pushed through it.

Marketing my book is still my least favorite part of the process, but I am getting better at it. I know how much my story has helped other people and I know I need it to find the right people; the people who need to read it. Looking at it this way has helped me push through the uncomfortable moments. My story is worth reading, and I am worth sharing it with others. Self-love isn't just important for the writing process, but for always.

Don't give up on yourself or sell yourself short. If the thought of asking strangers to buy your book is terrifying in the beginning, pick something small to work on. Start out by asking friends and acquaintances if they'd be interested in buying your book. When you get a little more courage and self-confidence, you can move your way up to standing in the middle of a bookstore in the city at Christmas time. You don't even have to do that, just do what feels comfortable and push yourself a little outside your comfort zone. You'll be surprised to see the changes in yourself as you become more comfortable talking about your book.

Since that time in the middle of a Barnes and Noble I have been to multiple readings and spoken at events. I was even a guest on the Dr. Phil show! When you push yourself a little, a lot of amazing things can happen. The best one of all is you'll begin to believe in yourself.

Your Author Platform

Another way to get yourself out there is to have an online presence. This can be done in many ways and is something you should focus on as soon as you know you want to publish a book. The first thing I did when I knew I wanted to tell my story was start a blog. There are many ways to do this, I started mine for free at https://wordpress.com/. A quick search online will yield multiple results for other free blog options.

When I started my blog, I made up a name for it and didn't share who I was. At first, I just wrote and didn't share it with anyone. When I was further along in my writing process, I purchased a domain name with my name and began sharing my posts on my personal Facebook page.

If you plan on using your name, or you know what your penname will be, it's a good idea to purchase the domain name, even if you're not ready to post, just so you're sure it will be available when you need it. You don't have to add blog posts to your site if that's not something you're interested in. Your domain can become your website where you can add information about your book and your contact information. Having a website that is easy for people to find will give you credibility as an author and can help you sell books.

After I was writing blogs for a while, I started my Facebook author page. Ironically, my mom was my first fan. When I started my page, I had no clear idea what I was doing, and I was at the stage where I didn't want anyone to know who I was. The name of my page was

Moonlit Madness, which was going to be the title of my memoir. It took me three years to change the name to my name and start building the audience.

If you're not sure you want to put your name out there, you can start the page with a penname or any title. Over time, if you decide you want to use your own name it's as simple as going in and changing your name. The idea is for readers to get to know you. The real you. They want to get to know about your life and things you enjoy. Once they trust you and feel like they know you, they will want to read your book. Offer helpful information, recipes, positive sayings, review other memoirs, post photos of your pets or anything else you feel like sharing. When you offer helpful and thoughtful content, your audience will grow.

The next thing I did was I started an Instagram and Twitter account. I tried to keep them active. Other authors use Pinterest, TikTok, Snapchat and have YouTube channels, but I was having a hard time with the ones I was already using. When I became overwhelmed with the amount of time it took me to focus on my social media presence, I decided to focus on my Facebook author page and my website. I do post on my other platforms, but I felt being good at one was better than being mediocre at all of them. It takes a lot of time to put yourself out there but if you put some time aside a few times a week, it will become manageable. Don't try to do it all, unless you want to and enjoy it. Have fun with this. You never know who might be watching you!

There are also a few author and reader online communities that are important for you to be active on.

The top three are Goodreads, BookBub and Amazon. These are platforms you can join before your book is published and after your book is out, you can add your own author profile. Interact with other authors and readers and leave reviews for the books you have read and enjoyed. I would suggest if you didn't love or like a book to skip the review. This profile will be linked to your author account and you don't want readers or authors seeing you be too harsh to other authors. You don't have to lie, just don't offer your two cents if you have nothing nice to say. You will get back what you put out, like the saying goes, you'll attract more bees with honey.

Find the platforms that will work best for you and start with one at a time. Follow other authors and watch what they do. Try not to be overwhelmed by all the options that are available to use and be prepared for more to be added that will become the next big thing. I found it hard to keep up with the changing social media craze and stopped letting it stress me out. I do what I can and I try to use my time to help connect with readers and other authors that want to interact with me. There are so many tools available to get your book and yourself into the writing community. Take it one post at a time and learn as you go.

Reviews and Critics

Now that your book is out in the world you will hear from readers, and even people who haven't read your book. Some reviews you receive will encourage you while others may crush you. I remember feeling my heart race up into my throat when I saw my first review had come in. I was so excited to see what people thought, but it also scared me to hear it. When I was notified of the review, I picked up my phone to read it and set it down as fast as I had picked it up. Fear of what I was about to read forced me back under the covers. The self-doubting narrative poured in and took over my every thought. My mouth went dry and sweat beaded around my hairline.

When the thoughts became too much for me to bear, I picked up my phone and clicked on the review. It was good. It was actually better than good; it was amazing. Tears welled up in my eyes as I reread the words the reviewer left. I pushed the self-doubt out and replaced it with self-confidence. The good news was people loved my book; it was helping them. The bad news was some people didn't love my book, they didn't even *like* it.

I had received over fifty five-star reviews before the first three-star review arrived, and when I read the harsh words from the review, it was all I could focus on. The kind and inspiring words from the other reviews remained in the background as the critical words became how I saw my story. I beat myself up over the criticism and even considered taking my book down. "But what about what all the other readers have told you? You've helped so many people, don't let it get to you." My husband's wise words helped me see the reality of it.

The kind words were important, too. They mattered as much as the harsh words. If I let one person's opinion cancel out all the others then I wasn't listening. I was so eager to agree with the negativity because I had been so used to believing those things about myself for so long. I was so used to believing my story didn't matter. But it matters. And thankfully I was able to realize that not everyone will like my story. Everyone is entitled to their opinion and their opinion is just that, theirs.

Taking constructive criticism is one thing. To become the best writer you can be you have to be open to listening to advice and tips that will help you grow and improve your craft. But listening to people be mean and judgmental is something entirely different. This will happen. It is a matter of when and not if. There are people out there that just want to destroy you and make you feel bad for no other reason than to be mean. There are also people who just won't like your style of writing or the concept of your book. And you know what? It's okay. Their opinion of you doesn't define you, don't let it take the wind out of your sails. Some of the best advice I was given (and don't always take) was to not read the reviews. They are for the readers and not for the author. Some people I have worked with have a friend check the reviews and only pass along the positive ones. Find something that works for you.

When you put your book out into the world, it becomes out of your control whose hands it falls into. It may sting when a stranger leaves a nasty comment in response to your book, but it can hurt even worse when someone you love has unkind things to say. My sister was upset with me about a few things I wrote and challenged me about some of my memories. It upset me at first, but we were able to talk about it and worked through the tension. Luckily (or unluckily depending on how you look at it) most of the people in my book were dead. I didn't have to worry about what they would say if they read about themselves.

You may have family members or friends who will not be supportive of you. They may even stop speaking to you or become angry with you for sharing the family's secrets. They might remember the story differently or they're not ready for the world to know. Be prepared for some unkind words or actions from people you love or care about. Know that some people will never be ready for your success. Those people are not your people.

Many of the people I have helped write their stories have reported back something equally painful. For many of them, their friends and family didn't acknowledge their accomplishment. One woman spent decades working on her story, and when it was published all she heard were crickets. After talking with her more we discovered the person who was being the least supportive had her own story to tell and it upset her friend that she had reached her goal before she did. It's hard to be attacked by people we love and it's also hard when they don't want to celebrate with us.

It's hard to say how others are going to react, just be prepared for anything. Expect a few unkind things to be said or written about you or your work. Know in your heart that you have done your best and don't let the harsh words from strangers or people you love hurt you. I know it's easier said than done, but I've been there, and I know you can do it. Don't let it destroy all the hard work you have done.

When you put yourself out there, it can be frightening. Once your story is out in the world, there is no more hiding. There are no more secrets to hang on to. Take time to embrace the vulnerability. The fear dissipates in time as you welcome your newfound power. Listen closely, can you hear it? That's your voice. Isn't it beautiful?

You've done a lot of hard work, and that work will live on for future generations to find. Your story could be someone else's survival guide. How awesome is that? Everything you went through to get you to where you are today could potentially save someone from having to experiencing what you went through. Your words may be all it takes to let someone else know they are not alone. Writing your story is a gift you give to yourself, but also to the people who read it.

Power Hint: Pick one social media platform you enjoy using and create an author page. Have fun with it and start building your audience.

Power Prompt: If someone were to ask you what your most important life lessons have been, what would you say? And why?

10

Helping others

> *"Success isn't about how much money you make, it's about the difference you make in people's lives." ~Michelle Obama*

Now that you are finished writing your story and you are on your way to having a published book, now what? What do you do with yourself now that the words are out of your head and onto the paper? What happens when your story is out in the world for others (maybe even strangers!) to read? After my memoir was published, I wasn't sure what to do with myself.

At first, I felt like a phony. After my memoir was on the printing press, I thought I had to be healed. I thought if I had told my story there was nothing left for me to do with my healing. At book signings and readings, I felt like

I had to be this healthy, healed person. I didn't think I could be anxious or nervous before readings. I felt I had to be an expert in my recovery.

Depression and self-doubt crept back in as I watched myself slowly fall back down. I wanted to hide from the spotlight, because I didn't feel like I was who people thought I should be. The idea that once the words left me, I would no longer be affected by them. I thought I would go from haunted to heroine with the printing of my book.

I continued going to counseling and Reiki, but didn't feel I should still be working on the issues I addressed in my book. I was supposed to be healed. I was supposed to be over it. After I exposed all the trauma I had kept hidden most of my life, I assumed I had to be okay with it now that I shared it with the world.

I was wrong. Some of my most in-depth healing came after my memoir was finished. Writing my story didn't automatically fix everything, but it helped me find my voice. My healing did not stop just because I put my pen down. I learned a lot about myself, maybe even as much as I learned during the writing process as I did after my book was finished.

Four months after my memoir was published, I found myself on the stage of the Dr. Phil show where I was able to confront my stepfather for the years of sexual abuse. Without taking the needed steps on my healing journey and getting the words out of my head and heart, and onto the page I never would have been able to do this. This experience helped move me along my healing path and allowed me to see things from a different perspective.

People reached out to me after they read my book and after they saw me on the Dr. Phil show. They shared secrets with me that they said they had told no one else. I was happy to help, and I was glad they found some comfort in the pain I had shared, but I couldn't receive their compliments. I listened graciously and responded with emails, thanking them for reaching out while assuring them it really hadn't been that big of a deal. The old script I had said to myself returned.

When I was able to crawl out from under the blanket of depression long enough to notice this, I brought it up to my counselor. She asked me how it felt to finally have my memoir published. With tears running down my cheeks, I told her I was a failure. I told her I wasn't healed. A smile spread across her face as she handed me a box of tissues. "You think?"

I didn't understand. I thought I had to be. I felt like in order to share my story, I had to be in a place in my life where I didn't let anything get to me. I had to be almost superhuman. I was wearing a cape now. It had to mean something. It did, but just not what I thought. True healing never ends. It is something we do every single day.

Depression slips back in and knocks me off my feet, but I don't give up. I keep on going. I go back to the self-care activities, making them a part of my everyday life. I go for a walk and have a cup of tea and I allow myself to feel what comes at me. If I slip up or get too busy to take care of myself, I pick back up where I left off. No one is ever done with their work.

This is when I really took hold of my power. This is

when I was able to help other people tell their stories. I slowly took the reins of my power and adjusted my cape. Writing your story will not fix all your problems, but it will give you the strength and foresight to continue on the healing journey.

Just because you have completed your story doesn't mean you should stop taking care of yourself. Take time for yourself every day, even if it's just a couple of minutes. Keep pushing the negative self-talk out of your head. Continue writing in your journal and unload all of your burdens from the day and all the joyful moments. If you have a bad day, brush yourself off and start over the next day. You're not perfect, nothing you can do will ever get you to that level but guess what… it's okay! Who wants to be perfect, anyway? That's too much pressure. Just be you. Be someone you can be proud of. And love yourself.

Do you want to help others with your story?

One of the primary purposes for writing my memoir was to help others. I wanted what I went through to be for something. If I could help someone else see that they were not alone, it was worth it for me. I knew my story had a lot of pieces to it, and most likely no one could relate to all of it, but I knew there were people who knew the pain I had felt. I knew I wasn't the only one who longed for a mother's love or was sexually abused as a child. I knew there were countless others who were survivors of domestic violence. Maybe they couldn't relate to all of it, but I knew there was enough to let many people know they were not alone.

When I was growing up, I felt alone. I didn't know other people lived without love from their mothers. I didn't know I wasn't the only one who learned about sex from inappropriate older males. I had no idea there were other people who left one abusive household to create one of their own. It was incredibly lonely, and I felt broken.

When readers began reaching out to me, I felt like I belonged. There were others who knew and had experienced the pain I had. When I released my secrets, I didn't only reclaim my power and find my voice, I also became part of a tribe. A tribe I had no idea existed before I wrote and shared my story.

Survivors sent me messages and emails. They shared stories they had told no one else. They let go of burdens that had been weighing them down. For some, that was all that they needed, but for others they wanted to learn how to share their stories, too. It took a while to understand I had all I needed to help others get release from their secrets, but once I realized all I needed to do was share what I knew and hold space the magic began to happen.

Think about what you want to come from sharing your story. Are you ready, maybe even excited to have your story reach other people who know what it's like? Or does the thought scare you a little (or a lot)? If you're nervous because you feel like you don't have what it takes, don't worry, you will. Everything you will need will come to you. Embrace the compliments and the comradery. You're not alone anymore, and this might be just what it takes to prove it to yourself.

Do you want to help others share their story?

The first time I helped someone else share their story, the freedom I had felt when I let go of mine returned. The powerful feeling of being more than what had happened to me multiplied. I witnessed other people take their life back from their trauma and find their voice. People who had not held their head up high in decades were walking tall, and it was because they had their freedom back. They had reclaimed their power.

The first writing class I taught turned into a support group after our scheduled time ended. After weeks of spending time together and hearing each other's stories, we developed a bond. We were not just writers, but we were also survivors. We celebrated each other's accomplishments and held space when we were feeling weak. The age of the participants ranged from mid-thirties to early eighties, but everyone became friends. The writing group turned support group turned into a small, close family.

Although our traumas were different, we had all known pain. We had all known heartache, neglect and abuse. Each one of our lives had been silenced because of the secrets we had held. Trauma had changed us, but it did not stop us. Even the oldest member in the group said she felt like a changed woman. I knew then that it is never too late to release the secrets. It's never too late to reclaim your power.

When I saw that others had reacted the same way I had after telling their stories, I wanted to help as many people as I could share their stories. I wanted to give as many people as I could the opportunity to reclaim their power and find their voice. Think how much power is out there waiting to be reclaimed. The more voices that are found, the louder they become.

Do you feel like you want to help others find their voice, too? Once you write your story, people who want to be where you are will look up to you. All you need to do is offer space and encouragement and you could become the reason someone else reached their dream. It really is that simple. What do you have to lose?

Ways to help others share their story

If you are inspired to help others share their story, you can start small. Have conversations with the people you love and ask them if they have a desire to share their story. Share with them how it helped you and offer some pointers you learned along the way.

If you want to help others, but not people you know, consider starting a writing group. You can do this online or in your community. It doesn't have to be anything fancy, just a place for people to come together and write. A group that I started a few years ago is still going strong. We meet a couple times a week and share things we have been working on, and also visit and check in with each other.

Now that you've learned the P.O.W.E.R. method, I hope you refer to it when you feel your voice slipping away. I'd love to tell you that once you release your story, all of your problems are solved forever and ever, but I'd be lying. I know, I was so disappointed when I found this out, too!

After I wrote the first draft of my story, before I shaped it into the memoir I published, I thought I had found the secret to a trauma free life. I assumed once I let go of all my secrets and addressed all the issues I had experienced, my work would be done. I thought it was a onetime deal. I could wash my hands of it all and skip away into the sunset with a cheesy, happy grin on my face.

Disappointment struck when that didn't happen. Don't get me wrong, the changes that happened in me since writing my story have been monumental. I found my voice after over thirty years without it. I learned to be gentle with myself and honor my past. If you met me before I started my writing journey, you'd definitely see the difference. I hold my head up when I walk now and I enjoy helping other people share their stories. It's my passion. It's what sets my soul on fire. But, I also fall back into my old thinking from time to time.

The thing is, the job of self-love and acceptance is never done. Most of us have lived with years of trauma and secrets that controlled our lives and stole our power. That doesn't just go away after a few months of making changes, but it gets easier. A big part of the process is knowing it's okay to not be okay all the time. Life is hard, it's not all sunshine and rainbows. Things happen that are out of our control.

The biggest lesson that I took away from this process was that I wasn't a failure because I was sad, or angry, or had a bad day. When depression settled over me like a weighted blanket, I didn't throw everything I had accomplished away. Sure, in the moment it's so easy to forget how far I had come but that didn't last. The tools I gathered along the way were still available for me to use. I also didn't hide these moments from others. I wrote blogs about these feelings because I wanted other people to know it was normal. We are often our own worst critics, but we can also be our biggest supports. We can have it all, the discouragement and the encouragement. We're complicated creatures!

My advice for you is to keep on going. When you feel like giving up, remember all that you've been through and all you have accomplished. Use your voice. Hold your head up high. You've worked hard to reclaim your power; you don't have to give it back.

Remember to rely on the foundation you built. If you feel stuck or need extra support, reach out for it. Pick up your journal and let go of what you're hanging onto. You don't have to hold on to it anymore. Continue trading out the negative self-talk and replace it with positive. You deserve a safe place to live, and that includes your own head.

Honor yourself with acts of self-care every day. Just because you're finished with your story doesn't mean you have to stop taking care of yourself. Find something you enjoy, even if it's small. Read a book you enjoy, drink a cup of your favorite tea, take a bubble bath or go back to the list you made and pick a self-care activity you know you can (and will) do that won't add stress to your life.

Celebrate your accomplishments

Now that you've written your story, even if you don't plan on publishing it, or even sharing it with anyone, make sure you take time to celebrate your accomplishments. It doesn't matter how big or small it is, celebrate. You deserve to give yourself the recognition for being brave enough to dig in and uncover the things you've been hiding from. If no one else offers you a celebration or gives you praise, be okay with giving it to yourself. You are worth your own approval.

My hope for you is that you found some peace in the process of letting go of your secrets. I hope you were able to let go of whatever you've been holding onto and the weight of their burden has lifted off of your shoulders. I hope you can embrace the power you have reclaimed. And I hope when it's your time to leave this world you won't have a story lodged inside of your heart that keeps you from peace. Everyone deserves the chance to unleash their secrets.

I'd love to hear how your story is going. Use #Reclaimyourpowertellyourstory to share your progress!

Now it's time to go pick out your cape… you've earned it! Welcome to the club of superheroes who have taken their life back from the trauma, and who have found their voice. It's getting loud in here!

Say it with me... "I AM POWERFUL!"

Power Hint: Don't forget to celebrate your accomplishments.

Power Prompt: What objects tells the story of your life?

Acknowledgments

I owe thanks and gratitude to so many people for the birth or *Reclaim Your Power*. After I published my memoir, I heard from countless people who wanted to share their story. Their desire and the fear that stopped them helped me see the need for this book.

Thank you to all of the people who shared their stories with me, in writing or in person. Without seeing your joy and hope, I might not have known I needed to write this! Thank you for your courage and vulnerability.

Thank you to my husband and children who had to live with me while I brainstormed, outlined, and planned this book. The amount of pressure I placed on myself through the project oozed out into other parts of my life, making me less than enjoyable to be around.

Thank you to my rescue dog, Charlie, for providing me with companionship and making me get up once in a while to go for walks.

Thank you to the friends I have made in the writing

community that helped me learn along the way. A special shout out to the Coffee Queens!

Thank you to the early readers who provided feedback and encouragement. I am blessed to have each and every one of you on my team.

Thank you, Shower of Schmidt Designs, for taking bits and pieces from me to create the perfect cover! You are magic!

Thank you, Proofreading by the Page, for being an awesome editor and proofreader. I always look forward to hearing what you have to say!

And, last (but not least!), thank you, the reader, who has taken the first step in releasing your story and reclaiming your power. Remember, you are brave, and you are powerful. You have everything you need inside of you. Take it one word at a time. ***I am so proud of you!***

About the Author

Jessica Aiken-Hall, author of her award-winning memoir, *The Monster That Ate My Mommy* and the *Scope of Practice Trilogy*, lives in New Hampshire with her husband, three children, and three dogs. She is a survivor of child abuse and domestic violence and is a fierce advocate. Her mission is to help others share their story.

She has a master's degree in Mental Health Counseling, with over a decade of experience as a social worker. She is also a Reiki Master and focuses her attention on healing.

When she is not writing, she enjoys listening to Tom Petty, walking along the beach, looking at the moon, and watching murder shows.

To follow what she's doing next check out http://www.jessicaaikenhall.com.

> Don't forget to grab your copy of the Companion Workbook!!

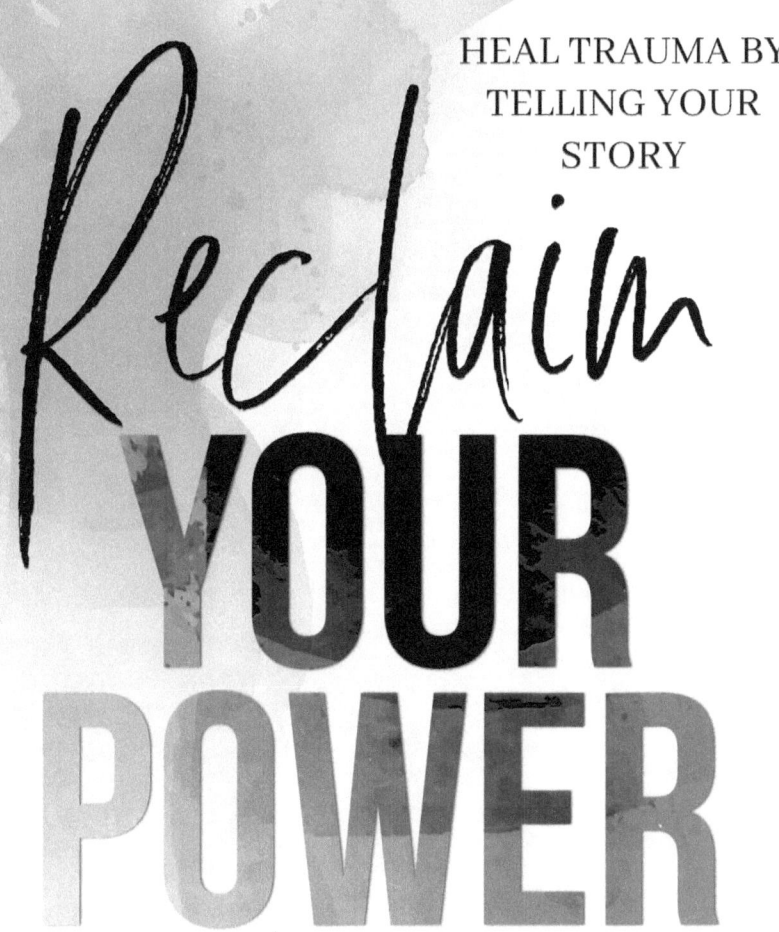

COMPANION WORKBOOK

HEAL TRAUMA BY TELLING YOUR STORY

Reclaim YOUR POWER

JESSICA AIKEN-HALL

www.ingramcontent.com/pod-product-compliance
Lightning Source LLC
Chambersburg PA
CBHW021425070526
44577CB00001B/60